# What This Book Can Do for You

Mental Cybernetics does not promise something for nothing. However, it promises something for something— namely, a far greater measure of everything that is good in life for those who will work with the particular tools of mind given you in this book. In its pages, you will find scores of mental processing techniques woven into an unfailing system that you can use to program your life for success in any fields you desire.

*The Science of Mental Cybernetics* was written for the increasing number of people in our world today who like to think—indeed, who insist on thinking constructively and concretely. It was not written for those who are content to dream without taking corresponding action, nor for those who expect others to do their thinking for them. This book shows the way to attain greater achievement, happiness, creativeness, self-confidence, and abundance for anyone who is willing to put his mind to work as described in its pages.

This book explains and demonstrates how your mind may be programmed—similarly to programming a computer—for success in any desired field, and what you can do to start immediately. Everyone's mind is actually a programmed mind, regardless whether a person lives in a hovel or a palace. Through the years, the thoughts, beliefs, desires, and attitudes fed as input into a person's computer-like mind, add up to produce the level of attainment where he finds himself to be. But, there is something he can do about it if he does not like where he so finds himself. He can reprogram his mind for desired success —the definite techniques you will find in this book.

Throughout the following pages you will learn how to monitor and screen out of your life any undesirable mental elements that prevent success. For example, Chapter Eight deals with negative hypnotic influences that may surround you, causing patterns of recurring failures to repeat themselves in your experience—and what you can do to free yourself from these frustrating forces.

In each chapter you will find mind-processing "input" cards to use for specific results you want. Affirm the dynamic message on these mental computer cards until they become engraved on the memory record of your mind. If you faithfully use them as set out in this book, they will raise the tone of your conscious and subconscious thinking, and that tone will help produce superior results in terms of desired attainment, happiness, serenity of mind in all situations, and success in producing the objects of your desires.

This book can awaken you to the vast new realm of achievement awaiting you as you tap the powers and potentials that are hidden or latent within the structure of your mind. There is no claim that the lives of all who read these pages will be magically transformed. However, I do know through the experience of myself and countless others that if you will study these mental programming techniques, incorporate and work them into your thinking process, they will work to produce significant changes which will benefit you greatly. For those who want an attractive new world of satisfying achievement for themselves, I say to you, all this is a present possibility for you and will flow from your application of the science of mental cybernetics as set out in the pages which follow.

*R. Eugene Nichols*

# CONTENTS

*How To Use Mental*
*Cybernetics for Success*
*in Any Field*

A blaze of neon lights made the street as bright as noon-day. A flashing sign over the entrance proclaimed the casino to be the "Home of the Slots." Inside, a busy crowd pushed in and out of aisles lined with dozens of one-armed bandits. One matron stood solidly before two slot machines, plying first one and then the other with a quarter and pulling the handle. Periodically, with a tantalizing tinkle, one of the machines returned a few coins to reward her effort. Nonchalantly, she picked them up and fed them back into the slot hole. Her quarters were soon exhausted, and she strolled away to get more change and try another machine. She is typical of thousands who visit the gaming meccas of the world in the hope of beating the machines.

However, slot machines and other gambling devices such as mechanical "Twenty-one" tables are designed to return to the player a lesser amount than he has invested. The mechanism inside these devices is programmed in favor of the house, returning to it a profitable percentage. This the machines do with mechanical certainty. And, if a certain one gets out of order and fails in its designed role, the establishment quickly corrects the mechanical defect.

What does a slot machine have to do with the mind of man? Just this: It is a programmed device set to perform in a prescribed way. It does that for which its program calls. Very similarly, the mind of man can be programmed to produce specific results. It may be programmed to return to the individual desired percentages of happiness, health, supply, and the good things of life. However, while some minds are programmed to pay off abundantly, others are designed merely to break even, and still others are set to lose.

Is it a matter of chance or luck that one person is born to lose, while another breaks even, and still others hit the jackpot? Certainly not! *If an individual has been playing the game of life without ever hitting the jackpot, it is due to the set of his mind.* And, if the mind has been set to lose, it can be reprogrammed to pay off abundantly in all that constitutes the *good* of life.

### The abode of man is mind

The abode of man is mind. It is in mind that man lives, and it is to mind that man must look for the solution to personal and collective problems. The set of the mind is reflected outwardly as experience. The science of mental cybernetics helps you understand the inner workings of your mind and gives you the steps you may take to reset your mind to produce success in the world.

Man is a product of mind and of what mind has achieved through eons of time. The separation of mind and matter—of cause and effect—is no longer tenable. The quip that was once heard on the college campus rings untrue today.

"What is mind?" a quizzical student would ask his companion.
"Never matter," came the pert reply.
The first student then countered, "What is matter?"
"Never mind," was his companion's retort.

This wordplay may have delighted the ear but it breached the truth. Mind and matter are related. They are ends of the same continuum. Mind flows into form ceaselessly, and this it does by means of a dependable law—a law of mental cybernetics.

# What is cybernetics?

First, what is cybernetics from a technological viewpoint? When you set the thermostat in your home to a desired temperature and the thermometer falls below that point, a mechanism is triggered causing the furnace to come on—that is cybernetics. When the pilot of a plane, after climbing to the desired height, sets an automatic pilot which maintains the plane on its course—that is cybernetics. The automatic gyrocompass used to steer ships, the control system used to direct antiaircraft fire, the automatically controlled oil-cracking stills developed by the petroleum industry, and the ubiquitous computing machine—all these involve the science of cybernetics.

Cybernetics in technological achievement is comparatively new, but as a principle it is as old as life. For example, up to the present time only a few men have orbited the earth. They are pioneers in space flight. They have experienced sensations never before experienced by other human beings. Yet, as pioneers they did not make it alone; a vast history lies back of them. The rockets and fuel that put these men into space, the computers, communication lines, and other specialized apparatus used underwent a long period of development and testing. Simulations of launching, orbiting, tracking, and recovery were performed thousands of times prior to the first man's entry into space. Success was assured, insofar as was humanly possible, before the first man was sent aloft. This success was due to the dependability of law—law that is as old as life itself. That law will repeat its performance under like conditions, and this it will do consistently and dependably.

Like cybernetics in the technological field, cybernetics in the mental field is relatively new, but as a principle it has always existed. Mental cybernetics is based on the consistent and dependable way mind works. The working of man's mind is a mystery that has long fascinated him. He has experimented with it and tested it. At last, to a large degree, the operation of mind has been reduced to applied laws that can be used with the assurance of success. The science of mental cybernetics is the system by which you can use these laws of the mental world.

# The creative nature of mind

Archimedes, the Greek mathematician of the third century B.C., boasted that if he had a lever long enough and a fulcrum stable enough, he could move the world. Although you may have no desire to move the world literally, there doubtless are situations and conditions in your world of experience that you would like to move. If so, there is a way to apply Archimedes' principle to those conditions of life that you desire to move out of your circle of experience. The lever that is long enough to move your life into other channels of creative action is *thought*. The fulcrum that is stable enough to bring about such a movement is *law*—the immovable law of universal mind.

The nature of thought is creative. The inventor uses thought as the lever with which he probes into matter and creates the new synthetics and products now coming to the market. Thought is a lever, but it is effective only when used with the fulcrum of natural law. The inventor who ignored the law of mathematics and physics would create failure in spite of all the thoughts that stirred within him. The research chemist who did not base his work upon the laws of chemistry would create naught but chaos.

You may be sure of this, however! No matter whether mind is creating success or failure, it is still creating. It is not a question of whether you shall create or not. It is only a question of *what* you shall create.

The successful research scientist uses the laws of physics as the fulcrum for his thinking. You can become a mental scientist and use the laws of mental cybernetics as the fulcrum for your personal thinking. When you do, you will be able to control successfully *what* you create.

## As you think, so you are!

A fundamental law of the science of mental cybernetics, simply stated, is this: *As you think, so you become.* "As a man thinketh in his heart, so is he." The law of mental cybernetics produces results for you according to the tenor, the intention, and the direction of your thinking.

16

Even when there seems to be no direction to thought, the movement of life flows through you at your level of understanding.

Archimedes spoke of a lever that is long enough. For your thought to be effective as a lever, it must be big enough. Each individual is a thinking center in mind. Like containers of water dipped from the ocean, any difference is one of degree, not of kind. Your mind, like the principle of mind found universally around you, is creative, unlimited, and exhaustless. Any difference between your mind and the infinite potential of mind tapped by inventors, composers, painters, and men of genius through the ages is only one of degree. You are not *all* of universal mind, but you are expressing that *allness* at your level of understanding. And you can learn to express more of that allness through a new kind of bigger thinking.

For example, a gallon of water would be a larger embodiment of the ocean than a pint, and a fifty-gallon barrel would be a larger container than a gallon, yet both would partake of the ocean in essence. You partake of mind when you think, but what size are your thoughts?

Picture in your imagination a large lake high in the mountains. Extending from this lake are numerous pipelines. Some of these pipes are one-half inch in size, some three-quarters, others are an inch or two in diameter, while some are great water mains. Imagine that these pipelines are designed to irrigate farm land spreading out in the valley below the lake. For the land to produce, the water must continue to flow. If a line ceased to carry the necessary water, you would not conclude that the lake had gone dry, especially if you could see lush vegetation at the terminals of the other pipelines drawing upon the same lake. You would know that sediment, or some kind of blockage, had stopped the flow of the life-giving water.

Your life is like that. There is one universal mind—one infinite ocean—from which your life flows. But boundlessly transcending the analogy of the lake, the reservoir of universal mind is limitless. The only limitation which exists is the size of the individual channel man provides to that infinite reservoir. If the amount of the flow through the channel is small, like the half-inch pipeline that is easily clogged by a few grains of sediment, the flow of the ocean of mind cannot nourish the life of that individual. What kind of sediment can block the line? In terms of thought, it is fear, doubt, self-depreciation, and false concepts regarding yourself and your creative nature that clog the flow of mental power.

The urge within you to create a good life arises from universal mind—that mind which is being individually differentiated by you. The difference between you and another is one of degree and not of kind. You can increase the degree of good you are experiencing by clearing out self-doubts and retraining your mind to think new thoughts about yourself. Get an idea that is big enough! Reprogram your mind with data that defines the person you want to be. All that you will ever need to move your life into more constructive paths of power and accomplishment is a long enough lever of thought—a thought that is correctly programmed for the good you wish to

> I now discard all self-doubts and frustrations, leaving them behind in a yesterday that is forever gone. I bring to this moment a new image of myself that refreshes every thought about my abilities. I now stand mentally tall and confident of the powers within me. I now see myself superbly fulfilling each task of today.

*Mental Data Processing Card No. 1*

demonstrate. Let the fulcrum for that thought be the first law of mental cybernetics: *As you think, so you become.*

Take a moment now to feed this new data into your mind. Reprocess your thoughts by reading Mental Data Processing Card No. 1 slowly with a deep, genuine feeling that the words describe the true you:

## How the nondiscriminating nature of mind works

From observation it would appear that there are vast differences in the blessings that come man's way. Individuals vary greatly in the degree of power, ability, and understanding they display. Many take for granted that certain people are naturally blessed with more power and a richer measure of abundance than others. This seems to imply that the universe shows favoritism. Yet I submit that the same wisdom and the same supply belong to each and all alike. True, there are wide gradations of talent and ability, but the difference is in what has been accepted and not in what has been given.

To understand the laws of mental cybernetics, you must see the relationship between the universal potential of mind and the individual's use of it. During the summer months, thousands of sunbathers avail themselves of the beaches along the shores of our land. Individually they soak up the rays of the same sun that shines on everyone. There is no hue and cry that some swimmers have been given more sun than others, yet one may have a deeper tan than another. It's not because the sun showered him with special blessings, but because he exposed himself more to the sun's rays. He has individualized his use of the sunshine through choice, just as all people individualize the use of mind power through the choice of their own thoughts.

Still another swimmer may choose to use an umbrella or to sit in the shade. This is his choice. The sun is available, but if the individual does not seek its rays, he will remain untanned. The sun does not care whether the individual sits in the shade or absorbs its warmth. Whether it is winter or summer, whether thousands are luxuriating on the sand or the beach is empty, whether a cloud momentarily cuts off the sunshine or the sky is cloudless, the sun keeps shining in all its impartial splendor.

Universal mind power is available to you on this same impartial basis. As a great teacher of long ago said, "He makes His sun rise on the evil and on the good, and sends rain on the just and on the unjust alike." In the spring the lilacs breathe their fragrance into the air for all. At night the stars send forth their radiance for the wonder of all beholding eyes. Everywhere life gives of itself to all individuals, regardless of their persuasion or intent. It is the purpose of the science of mental cybernetics to show you how you can tap the power of mind that is impartially awaiting your use to produce a constructive life of health, happiness and success.

Just as one sunbather can bare his body to the sun's rays and receive a deeper tan, so can the individual expose himself to a universal mind power and receive richer blessings. Each person has the freedom to move from his present position, if the view from it is not pleasant and life-enhancing, to a new position in mind. With the use of this science, you can move from the shade into the sun—from a negative of passive consciousness into a state of mind that demonstrates success and fulfillment.

Of course, the individual can choose to remain in the shade, but he also has the freedom to move into a new awareness, a new position in consciousness. This will not give him more wisdom or more power, for all wisdom and all power have been given, but it will expose his life to a higher consciousness of that which is latent within him now.

## How mental cybernetics can work for you

With the use of mental cybernetics, you can step out of the shade of negation and false programming of mind into the light of affirmative living. If you have been existing under an umbrella of self-depreciation and failure, it is time to use the principles set forth in this book to help you to a new life. It is time to realize that the responsibility for a change in your life lies in what you choose to think about yourself, for mind itself is impartial. This brings us to a second fundamental law of mental

20

cybernetics: *Through your freedom of choice you tap and direct the impartial power of mind.*

Like the sunbather exposing himself to the rays of the sun which shines for all with impartial splendor, you must open your life to greater good through the wiser direction of your thoughts. This you can do (a) by a realization of the power that is available to you, (b) through a realignment of attitudes, (c) by an awareness of the forces motivating your life, (d) through dehypnotizing yourself of false beliefs and false programming concepts, and (e) by erasing old thought patterns with new data about yourself.

## Two sides to this science

Like a coin that has two sides, every science has two facets. In mathematics, there are the mathematician and the figures with which he works. In chemistry, there are the chemist and the elements with which he creates new synthetics. In mental cybernetics, there are the conscious you and the subconscious mind with which you create. Of course, the conscious you and your subconscious mind are not two separate factors like the mathematician and his figures. The conscious and subconscious sides of you are as inseparable as two sides of a coin. However, they are distinct in their functions, and it is these functions with which you must be familiar in order to use the laws of mental cybernetics.

### THE CONSCIOUS SIDE

Let's examine each side of the coin in turn. The conscious you is the planner of life. You have the privilege of consciously analyzing a situation, choosing alternative ways of behavior, and deciding on one of them. You have the conscious power to initiate new activity or to stop your present activity. In brief, the conscious you is mainly responsible for directing your life.

### THE SUBCONSCIOUS SIDE

What's the other side of the coin? What's the other

aspect of the dual nature of mind? It is the subconscious or inner mind. The subconscious mind supplies the know-how to carry out the directions of the conscious you. When the conscious you says, "It's time to stop lolling in bed and get up," it is the subconscious autonomic system that obeys, puts your feet on the floor, and flexes your muscles into an upright position. When you are consciously discouraged, you communicate a pessimistic tone to the subconscious. It, in turn, is depressed and lowers the tone of the body. When the conscious you is exuberant, a radiant tone is communicated to the subconscious, and you have one of those days when you feel that you can lick the world.

It is obvious that the subconscious mind in you is creative. It supplies energy. It supplies power. It supplies the know-how that builds and maintains the body. At the same time, however, it is suggestible to your conscious command. It is receptive to the direction you give it. Because it obeys you, you can train it. You have already trained it in dozens of ways—in habits you have developed, in skills you have acquired, and in reflexes that have become conditioned. You are using the suggestible nature of the subconscious when you train your fingers in the habit patterns of touch typewriting. You are also using the suggestible nature of the inner mind when you train yourself to react with set attitudes, preferences, or prejudices.

## The subconscious is a processing medium

The subconscious is a processing plant. As the stomach processes the food you eat into the elements that sustain physical life, so does the subconscious mind process the food of impressions fed into it. Acting upon data supplied by the conscious mind, upon attitudes and opinions, upon beliefs and half-truths, the subconscious converts your thoughts into things. Ideas and thoughts become processed by the subconscious into experience. The content of your thoughts directs your life toward success or failure, toward health or illness, toward love or loneliness.

Clearly, the subconscious is retentive. It retains the

data you program into it. It retains the image of yourself that you feed into it again and again each day. *And, by its very creative nature, it is obliged to mold you into your conscious image of yourself*. However, it is this very creative nature that is your hope of change. It is the medium by which you can bring a new self-image into manifestation.

Briefly now, remember that the conscious you is the director and the subconscious you is the doer. This is your dual mental nature. This is the coin with the two sides. In mental cybernetics terminology:

1. Conscious mind is the programmer—the initiator of action.
2. Subconscious mind is programmed—the medium of action.
3. Experience is the program output—the result of action.

Or, stated in another way:

1. Conscious mind is the observing self.
2. Subconscious mind is the serving self.
3. Experience is the service that is rendered.

### The dual nature of mind

During the past century, many attempts have been made to define the dual nature of man's mind. In the area of psychoanalysis, Sigmund Freud explored what he called the conscious and the unconscious mind. In the area of neurology, man has long been familiar with the operation of the voluntary (conscious) and involuntary (subconscious) nervous systems. Behavioral scientists such as John Watson have demonstrated how the subconscious mind can be conditioned to respond to conscious stimuli. All of this research has helped man to a better understanding of why he acts as he does.

Have you ever wondered why you do some of the things you do? It is because of the retentive and obedient nature of the subconscious mind. Somehow, sometime, you have conditioned it to react as it does. Some way, the volitional (voluntary, choosing, conscious) you has set the mechanical you in motion. Remember, your dual mind is the programmer and the programmed; it is conscious and subconscious; it is action and reaction. Like the two sides of the single coin that cannot be divorced one from the other, the mind must function as action and reaction that cannot be separated. Action is initiated by conscious mind whose function it is to envision, to plan, and to set the course of your life. The role of the subconscious is to accept, obey, create, retain as memory, and react in accordance with what has been initiated.

## MECHANICAL ASPECT OF MIND

These two functions of mind have long been recognized, and their function was clearly delineated by Thomas Jay Hudson who authored *The Law of Psychic Phenomenon* over 75 years ago. Of the mechanical aspect of mind he said, "The subjective mind is constantly amenable to control by the power of suggestion." Because of this suggestibility, the conclusion must follow that "the subjective mind is incapable of inductive reasoning. The meaning of this is that the subjective mind involuntarily accepts as veridical the ideals or statements of fact imparted to it." [1]

Hudson was among the first who foreshadowed what is known about mind today in mental cybernetics. The subconscious mind must accept involuntarily the data imparted to it. It must act on the statements programmed into it. Hence, it is a programmed mind, and, being deductive in its reasoning (deducing answers from the premise given it by the conscious mind), it has no recourse but to do that for which its program calls. When the conscious mind says "I am," the subconscious mind says "I do," and does it.

The discouraged person has a make-up of mind that invites experiences which evoke discouragement. Inadvertently, he has said to the subconscious, "I'm headed nowhere—accomplishing nothing in life," and the subconscious does its best to make the statement true! The person with a failure consciousness is conditioning himself to failure. The individual with a success-consciousness

24

is implanting an interior blueprint that calls for success.

The expression is common that "success begets success." This is true, for the inner mind must outpicture the input that has been fed into it. This explains the Bible passage that reads, "To him who hath shall be given, and from him who hath not shall be taken away even that which he hath." [2] He who has a success consciousness will demonstrate success. He who sinks into a failure consciousness will find the little that he had slipping from his grasp.

## Your personal mental computer

In the field of computer electronics, the programmer feeds instructions into the machine in exact, logical, and sequential form. Not everyone can be a good computer programmer. It takes someone who can understand the precise logic and order in which data must be arranged before it is presented to the machine for an answer.

Similarly, not everyone is a good programmer of his own computer-like subconscious mind. Often the data being fed into the subconscious is illogical and contradictory. How can two incompatible aspirations both be realized? How can conflicting desires fed into the subconscious both be demonstrated? Just as a computer rejects a keypunch card that has illogical, erroneous information on it, so the subconscious is stymied by illogical, incompatible desires.

It is a safe bet that the conscious-mind thoughts of the person who is getting nowhere, if keypunched and fed into a million-dollar computer, would bring the machine to a grinding halt. Likewise, the data he has fed into the subconscious has caused a million-dollar mind to end up with a dime.

In the technological programming of a computer, logical knowledge is necessary. There must be knowledge of what the machine is to do, the industry it is to serve, and the results that are desired. The same is true of mind. In the programming of mind, knowledge is necessary. There must be knowledge of what the mind is to do, the purpose it is to serve, and the results that are expected.

What does the program of your mind call for? Is it

designed to do the job you want it to do? Is it designed for happiness? Is it programmed for health? Does the blueprint of the subconscious call for abundance?

In cybernetics language, the proposition is simply this: The machine that is designed to mow grass, mows grass. Likewise, the mind that is programmed to dig ditches, digs ditches.

Remember how the one-armed bandit is set or programmed to pay off for the house? Well, you occupy the house position, and your mind is paying off for you according to its set. Is it set to return a profit or a loss?

### How to program a rich and meaningful life

How can you program your mind to pay off consistently for you in regard to those qualities and values that make life rich and meaningful? This is the way: As the programmer of your subconscious, decide now what the machine is to do, what consistent and logical desires it is to serve, and what the results are to be. Pause now and give this thorough consideration, using Mental Data Processing Card No. 2 to reprogram your inner mind with new, consistent desires about the life you wish to demonstrate.

I now give my life new direction. I am clear and consistent about the person I want to become. I recognize desires that are incompatible with success and I discard them. I choose with logic the steps that now lead me to the life abundant.

*Mental Data Processing Card No. 2*

### All people have programmed minds

In considering how the subconscious mind can become programmed or set for a certain return, no one is ex-

26

cluded. It is not a question of one mind being conditioned while another is free and spontaneous. Years of living have etched upon the subconscious of each person patterns of action and reaction. The backlog of belief, the conditions of life and the experiences encountered *all* make for individually designed minds. This does not deny the fact that there are also deeply subjectified patterns of a collective nature that are common to all.

The pattern of one mind may be preferable to that of another, but each has a programmed mind. Some minds are keypunched for unhappiness. And while it seems cruel to suggest to a chronically ill person that his mind is imprinted for illness, yet evidence of this is recognized by psychosomatic medicine.

Dr. Flanders Dunbar, in her book *Mind and Body,* has said: "In the hidden recesses of their minds they have even made a blueprint of the disease they want." She continued with the observation that "they select symptoms in much the same way healthy people select clothes, choosing carefully for style, fit and effect upon others. Yet many do not know that they have done it." [3]

The mind with a blueprint that calls for illness is not consciously aware of the fact. The individual whose mind is keypunched for failure is seldom cognizant of the negative self-image that has been fed into the subconscious. The person whose mind is blueprinted for loneliness is not aware that it is so patterned. And frequently the one whose mind is designed for success is not aware of the interior pattern that is imprinted with his success formula. Such a person thinks of it as natural to make money. He is the man who declares, "Everything I touch seems to succeed."

## How your beliefs govern your life

Your beliefs govern your life. This does not mean that you are the author of every belief and attitude that dominates your thinking. In fact, many of the beliefs you call your own may not have been originated by you at all. For example, beliefs that have molded your image of yourself may have sprung from another person's remarks about you. If you were belittled or criticized by others,

27

your belief in your own ability may have been crippled.

Many an unsuspecting individual has had nothing to do with his beliefs except to believe them. He did not originate them. He never stopped to analyze them, test them, verify them, or reject them. He has only believed them. Many ideas he calls his own had their first home in the mind of another. Or they may have evolved from the surrounding culture, environment, or mass consciousness. The collective thought of a society, accepted by the individual, comes forth as the output of experience in his life through the programmed action of the subconscious.

Emerson speaks of this collective habit-thought as *the conspiracy of society against the individual.* William James spoke of habit as the *flywheel of society.* He said, "It (habit) alone prevents the hardest and most repulsive walks of life from being deserted by those who tread therein." [4] You can break free of any station in life that *society* has assigned to you to the degree that you can become the author and originator of your own beliefs about yourself. You have trained the habit-forming nature of the subconscious to behave according to your present image of yourself—an image that may have been largely colored by another's remarks and criticism. Stop accepting belittling beliefs originating in outer influences around you, and retrain the habit-forming center within you to behave according to a new success image of yourself. Remember, whatever your walk of life may be, the path you tread is due to a corresponding program lodged in the subconscious mind.

## Steps toward self-direction

Stop now and ask yourself these questions—questions that the science of mental cybernetics will answer for you as you read on:

1. How is the mind programmed?
2. When was my mind stamped with the data that controls my life?
3. What purposes and objectives are punched into my program card?
4. By whom was my mind conditioned?

5. How can I reprogram my mind for greater success?

In the field of technology, man is making rapid advances in the development of the self-controlled machine. Some time ago he designed the automatic pilot used in the self-direction of aircraft. He has developed self-regulating devices for satellites and rockets. There is the possibility that self-repairing and maintaining factors may be programmed into machines that will bring technology to the point of perpetual motion. In fact, man may eventually outwit himself and create a self-controlled machine so perfect that he loses control of it himself.

Although such a possibility is fantasy, man has reached the moon and is on his way to the planets beyond. With each succeeding day, word is released of new marvels of mastery and control that rock the imagination. Yet, with all this progress and achievement, what has man done about the control of his own mind? The greatest unexplored field lies in the science of mental cybernetics and the mental laws that can help man find self-direction and self-control of the forces within him.

Through a right understanding of the nature of mind and its use in the achievement of desired goals, man can:

Learn how to program his mind for success.

Develop a new self-image through step-by-step mental processing.

Erase old thought patterns with new data about himself.

Become the person that he wants to be.

## CHAPTER SUMMARY OF POINTS TO PONDER

1. Mind is dual in its nature. It is conscious and subconscious. It is volitional and mechanical. It is the programmer and the programmed.

2. The conscious mind is the programmer, while the subconscious mind, being constantly amenable to control by suggestion, is the programmed.

3. The subconscious, being a programmed mind, must do that for which its program calls.

4. The subconscious mind operates like a pro-

29

grammed machine. A device such as the slot machine is set to pay off a percentage that will bring a profitable return to the house. It must behave thus for it is set this way. Likewise, the subconscious mind is programmed to return to the individual varying percentages of happiness, health, and success according to its *set*.

5. In computer technology, the programmer must give instructions to the machine in logical, consistent, sequential order if an answer is to be obtained. There must be definite knowledge of what the machine is to do, the industry it is to serve, and the results that are desired. In directing the personal computer of your subconscious, your commands must be clear and consistent. They must be compatible with success. They must agree logically with the results you wish to experience. Therefore, enlightened knowledge of the nature of mind, the purpose it is to serve, and the results expected are necessary.

6. The relationship between the two phases of mind described as the volitional (voluntary, self-choosing) and the mechanical is this: The volitional mind says, "I am," while the mechanical-computer nature of the subconscious says, "I do," and does it.

# CHAPTER TWO

*The Wonderful
World of You Through
Mental Cybernetics*

"Does my life have meaning," asked the man sitting across the desk from me, "and if so, what?"

I wanted to counter with, "What meaning have you given to life?" but I realized that to answer with a question would not suffice. John's plight was typical of the lives of many. He had tried numerous jobs and ended up in one that was dull and routine. It afforded an income but little creative satisfaction. He felt a lack of purposefulness.

Snow was falling gently against the windowpane, and, taking this as a cue, I asked my visitor if he had ever observed the beautiful pattern of a snowflake. They piled up in the corner of the window as I continued, "A snowflake is a perfect example of a designing principle that is inherent in life. Moisture gathers in the cold winter air, and something that was seemingly nothing becomes a geometrical six-pointed star—a marvel of design and beauty. The next moment it may be a drop of water and still later invisible vapor, but what of the principle that designed the pattern?"

John seemed curious, so I explained: All forms of life follow definite patterns of unfoldment. An organism, as it unfolds from a seed or an egg, moves steadily toward a mature individualized expression of life. Something within the snowflake gives it its unique pattern. Something in a grain of wheat makes it distinct from a kernel of corn. Let us simply call that something *cause*. It causes

31

wheat to be wheat. It causes corn to be corn. In that cause is lodged the principle of design and purpose. This cause permeates every part of nature and gives each thing its unique purpose and pattern.

Here was the point I wanted John to get, so I asked him, "If purpose and design belong to the nature of the universe, is it not reasonable to believe that the designing principle is also within man?" John nodded as I added, "The planner is not external, but internal. Life is an inside job. The purpose of life is within each of us. It is not something to be acquired but something to be realized and fulfilled. The purpose of life is to express the unique, special pattern latent in you."

Then I asked John the question that first came to my mind at the beginning of the interview, "What meaning have you given to life? What outlet have you given the unique creative pattern within you?"

"That's just it," countered John. "I don't seem to have any place to go. I have had a dozen jobs since school, and none of them seemed right for me. How can mental cybernetics help me?"

I asked John to describe himself to me. "Tell me about yourself. What kind of person are you?"

John began by saying, "Well, you can see for yourself that I'm six feet tall and weigh about 180 pounds."

I broke in, "I don't want a description of the box; tell me about the contents. I want to know about you, not about the wrappings. I want to know your self-image—your self-definition."

Seeing that this was something which he had not thought about before, I asked him to write a description of himself for our next interview. To help him formulate his description, we talked on for a time about what a self-image is and how it is formed.

## What is a self-image?

Do you have a family album? Remember those baby shots on the bearskin rug, the round-faced youngster, the gangling adolescent, and then the mature adult? Such snapshots and portraits are images of you, but they show only the wrappings. The real self-image is not the one pasted in the photo album but the one that has been etched on the microfilm of your subconscious mind.

If a snapshot of the round-faced youngster could capture his feelings as well as his freckles, a self-image would be something that could be seen. To the contrary, a self-image is an unseen composite of all of a person's inner feelings, attitudes, self-evaluations, and ratings. He started gathering this composite picture when quite young, and he adjusts it or confirms it each day. This inner album of belief constitutes the data with which he, as programmer, has programmed the subconscious mind. The individual cannot see his thought images, but, like the latent images on snapshot film, they are developed in the darkroom of the subconscious. In turn, these images are projected on the screen of daily experience as habit-reactions and set patterns of behaving.

These inner patterns of belief about the self may be ones of lack, loneliness, absence of security, or a deficiency in terms of self-worth. These images on the microfilm of the subconscious may be distorted. They may be hazy or clear. They may be overexposed, as with the person who overrates himself. They may be underexposed, as with the person who underrates his abilities. They may be double-exposed, as with the individual who super-imposes incompatible images upon himself in a struggle to please everyone. But whatever the quality of these images which constitute the inner microfilm library of thought, it is this composite that intrudes into one's daily behavior. This is one's self-image.

## The darkroom of the subconscious

It is curious that centuries before modern psycho-analysts began probing the darkroom of the subconscious for latent childhood images, the nature of what goes on in the subconscious was suspected. The story is told that the prophet Ezekiel, in a vision, heard these words: "Son of man, have you seen what the elders of the house of Israel are doing in the dark, every man in his room of pictures?" A man's picture room can be none other than the subconscious. To examine that picture room and to see what images have been stored there is the beginning of wisdom. It is also the beginning of change.

A person can better alter his self-image when he discovers what he is doing in the darkness of unknowing. What is he doing on the inner plane of belief? What pattern of self is he feeding into the creative mechanism of the subconscious? What is his mental self-image? The pattern of the oak tree sleeps in the acorn. A stalk of corn springs from the pattern in the kernel. The personality of man springs from his self-image. This is a patterned universe. There is an interior design for every outward effect. The experiences of your life are latent in the pattern formed by your beliefs and attitudes about yourself.

I asked John now to undertake a description of his self-image. He was instructed to search the darkroom of his subconscious to discover what he really believed about himself. He was to evaluate both his negative and positive qualities and make an honest rating of himself on personality factors, character traits, preferences, attitudes, and prejudices.

"Just how," John asked, "do you want me to make this rating?"

"List—one under the other—the positive and negative qualities that best describe you," I explained. "Then make three columns and rate the traits as strong, average, or weak." John agreed to try and was to bring his list to our next session together.

I wondered what John would recognize in the picture room of the subconscious. If he were honest with himself, it would be the beginning of wisdom, the beginning of change. I was curious to know what he really felt about himself.

### How to find a self capable of commanding your love

How do *you* really feel about yourself? Are you a person you like living with? It is a common admonition that you should love your neighbor as yourself. However, if you are to love your neighbor, you are required by the very nature of life to begin by loving your neighbor's neighbor—and that is you! The depth of your love for others will be gauged by whether or not you have found a self within capable of commanding your love.

To find this self that is worthy of your love is one of the primary aims of mental cybernetics. This science affirms the rightness of being interested in yourself. This does not mean that you ever disregard the worth of others. No man stands alone. Not only are you involved with others at social and economic levels, but there is kinship with others at the mental level as well. Mind power is everywhere present. It comes forth as each individual. Each person, thus, is an incarnation of this one universal mind principle which is common to all men.

The potential of universal mind in each is equal. It cannot be said that there is more principle of mind in one person than there is in another. However, it can be said that some people make outstanding use of the mind power within them. In the *use* of mind man stands alone, for each person must awaken individually to his own worth. No one can force wisdom upon you. No one can awaken to life's joy for you. *You* must awaken to your own worth and to that self which is capable of commanding your love.

### Recognizing the world of the self

In order genuinely to love your neighbor's neighbor (you) and to find that self which is capable of commanding your admiration, you must come to recognize the designing principle inherent in you. At the selfsame moment that you recognize this designing cause, you will also find purposefulness. You will grasp your own unique, special, personal worth.

What gives each man this special worth? It is life's ability to personalize matter. From distinguishing fingerprints to unique mental characteristics, no two individuals are ever exactly alike. The greatest mystery—the most wonderful mystery—in life is that of personal identity, personal mind, personal consciousness. Universal mind comes forth with unique individuality through every leaf, through endless varieties of flora and fauna, and through every member of this knowledge-seeking specie known as man. Every individual views life from his own personal position. Every person fills a role in life that can never be duplicated. This wonderful world of yours is yours and yours alone.

## Life is an inside job

Life seems to be an outward daily experience, but living is really an inside job. When you are at peace, you are the only one who can know the depth of that peace. When you are confused or lonely, you are the one who experiences the discord and loneliness you feel. When you are ill, you are the only one who experiences the pain and discomfort of that condition. When your body tingles to the tune of vibrant health, you are the one who enjoys the exhilaration of that state of being. Living *is* an inside job. Although daily experience seems tied to environment and the world around you, experience really begins in the world within you. It is here, in the world of the self, that your entire life takes place. That inner world will be a wonderful place once you recognize the unique, personal self which is worthy of your love.

## There will never be another you

In the lyrics of the songwriter, "There will never be another you." How true this is! The designing cause of the universe makes no two things alike. What are you doing with this original unique individuality that you are? Are you making the most of this wonderful world of you? Or, do you belittle yourself? Do you permit self-depreciation to rob you of your confidence? Do you compare yourself unfavorably with others? Do you envy others' possessions or seek to imitate their traits?

You never need to imitate for you, yourself, are an original. A gown that is of original design is worth more than a copy that is made from it. So it is with your life. You are cut from an original pattern. Discover and take pride in that genuine design and do not try to imitate others, for your attempts will be counterfeit. If you were to walk into a bank and try to cash a counterfeit bill, even if you were not aware of its spurious nature, it would be taken from you. It is the same in the "bank of life." The bank of life will honor the genuine currency that you are but not the counterfeit. Fake currency has no power to purchase anything that is real. A false, counterfeit personality cannot build lasting happiness and success.

No one else in all the world can do the things you can do, can do them as well, or in the way you can. There is an area of life that will be unfulfilled unless you fill it. Emerson implied that man must cultivate his own uniqueness when he observed:

> There is a time in every man's education when he arrives at the conviction that envy is ignorance; that imitation is suicide; that he must take himself for better or worse as his portion; that though the wide universe is full of good, no kernel of nourishing corn can come to him but through his toil bestowed on that plot of ground which is given to him to till.[1]

This is not to say that the "portion" given man is static or limited. The creative potentialities in that plot of soil are endless, unless man fails to till his plot. The point is that in order to merit the good of this wide universe, you must use your talents and use them in your own unique way.

Life is like a sparkling diamond with millions of facets. Each facet reflects the brilliancy of this universe of good in its own way. You are a facet of this "diamond of life." You are designed to reflect your portion from the special, unique place you occupy in the diamond. Without the radiance from the facet you are, the diamond is incomplete.

Universal mind has placed the stamp of individuality upon itself and called it you. You are you. You are unique. You are important. No one else is in competition with you, nor can anyone ever be. Seek to excel as the original that you are. You are not here to match your wit or skill with others and meet with defeat or victory. You are here to express life—to express creatively this unique design that you are.

Assert the uniqueness and individual expression of that mind which lives in you! Express through the window-of-you the beauty, the joy, and the abundance that is potential to you in that *wonderful world of you!* Let your light so shine that all may see the unique facet you are in the diamond of life!

## How to find the wonderful world of you

A week after John's original visit, he returned with his self-evaluation—his description of his self-image. "It is here that we shall begin," I explained. "We'll go over each trait and quality you have listed and see where your self-image may be counterfeit. I want you to identify the self-concepts that fall short of the wonderful, unique, special, original person you really are. Once identified, you will be able to discard these misconcepts."

John and I examined his list. He had been objective and honest enough to include some negative qualities. I advised him to start to work on the negative ones he had rated "strong." In place of these concepts that fell short of the uniqueness and dignity of his true self, new concepts had to be programmed into the subconscious. These new concepts took shape in John's mind as we talked together about the wonderful world of the self. They took shape also as he affirmed each day thereafter the data I wrote on a card for him to guide him in reprogramming his thoughts.

Every individual owes it to himself to improve that inner world of the self where his actual living takes place. That consciousness of self in which you live should be cleared of misconcepts and distorted self-images. Search the darkroom of your subconscious now and discard all concepts that fall short of the wonderful, original, unique, beautifully designed individual that you really are. To help you identify these misconcepts, write a description of yourself as John did. Down the left-hand side of a sheet of clean paper list, one at a time, the positive and negative qualities that honestly describe you. Then make three columns on the right-hand side of the sheet, and rate these traits as strong, average, or weak.

| DESCRIPTION OF SELF (Positive and negative traits) | STRONG | AVERAGE | WEAK |
|---|---|---|---|
| Impatient | X | | |
| Persistent | X | | |
| Imaginative | | X | |

Next, pick out the qualities that require attention—i.e., the strong negative traits and the weak positive traits. Replace such uncomplimentary images of yourself with new data. For each strong negative quality, envision a new positive one. For each weak positive quality, envision one that pulsates with new vigor and drive.

Pause now and read Mental Data Processing Card No. 3 several times. Say the statements with conviction. Say them and mean them! As you say them, let your mind be filled with an image of the new positive qualities you wish to demonstrate.

### You are a ruler of a limitless kingdom

It may hardly seem necessary to introduce you to anything so close and personal as the wonderful world of you, but how much do you really know about this kingdom? Do you know that you are its rightful king? Do you know how to take command? Are you aware that this inner kingdom is an inlet to all of the abundance of the universe?

I believe in my uniqueness. I believe that I am creative in a special and original way. I affirm that a constructive, purposeful design now moves through me and impels me to new success and fulfillment. Misconceptions fall away as I embrace the true concept of my self-worth and unique value to the world.

*Mental Data Processing Card No. 3*

39

Emerson said, "There is one mind that is common to all individual men. Every man is an inlet to the same and all of the same." [2] With your individual mind, you may tap and use all of the abundance, wisdom, wit, insight, and accumulated knowledge of the universe. All is at your command. Your rightful duty is to rule over this mental realm as king. The throne room of your life is the conscious mind, and the scepter of power resides in your thoughts and feelings. These thoughts and attitudes are the royal edicts proclaimed by the crown. They are carried out by the obedient servant of the subconscious mind.

Each individual is a being of two worlds. The first world is the mental realm of thought, feeling, and belief—that wonderful world of the self. The second world is the realm of outer effect where thoughts, attitudes, and beliefs make themselves felt as form and experience. The question may be asked, with which realm should man be more concerned? If he is to be realistic, which realm will he try to change? The outer world is not illusory, but its reality is that of effect. Both realms are real—one as the realm of *cause* and the other as *effect*. But in order to change the government of the outer state of affairs, man must work with the inner realm of cause where the original edicts have been issued.

It does little good to manipulate effects and attempt to change circumstances by eliminating symptoms. However, if you can get at the cause behind the symptoms, permanent change is possible. As a dweller of these two worlds—the mental realm of cause and the outer realm of effect and experience—most of your real work must take place in the first realm. Here is where you can change the thoughts and images that activate the subconscious mind. Here is where you can formulate the commands with which you may reprogram your life.

To use mental cybernetics effectively, you must become aware that some cause, direct or indirect, lies behind every effect. And, until that cause is changed, the effect that it manifests will continue to persist in some manner, shape, or form. Briefly, this rule of mental cybernetics states: *A law of cause and effect governs all creation.*

40

*To create anew, you must initiate new causes from which new effects will flow.*

Remember, in order to use this law, you must go to the inner mental kingdom of cause—that wonderful world of the self of which you are the rightful ruler. This is where the thought commands are issued that govern the kingdom. However, these thought commands can be no wiser than the ruler himself. If you, as the ruler, have thought deeply about life and its meaning, then the orders coming from the throne room of the conscious mind will operate as causes that bring constructive chains of events into your world. But if you, as ruler, act only from surface motives, acquired impulses, superficial reactions, and responses conditioned by time and experience, then your commands will be shallow and will deal mainly with effects.

Man is the focal point for the creative activity of life. He has the authority to speak and to accomplish according to the word spoken. All too often, however, the word man speaks as ruler is thoughtless and unwise. He may speak from a counterfeit self which is not genuine and sincere. He may speak from a surface self—a false, acquired self—that is filled with fear, with doubt, and with self-depreciation. Such words of self-condemnation are perjured testimony to the good of life. The irony is that the creative subconscious mind will obey man's words of command and will attempt to deliver to him according to the commands he has given—delivering him to bondage if his words call for prison or to freedom if his words speak of liberty.

### How to stop cheating yourself out of the good things of life

As ruler of his mental kingdom, man is always affirming some state of being for himself. He impels himself lifeward or deathward, depending upon the way he talks about his life. He may talk himself into success or failure, into courage or fear, into love or loneliness. His speaking is not his mere verbal utterances—not simply the sounds he strings together in English, French, German, or Watusi—but his unverbalized self-appraisal as well.

41

This self-appraisal is much like a musical composition. It is the tune man plays night and day. This never-ending tune, like background music piped into a modern reception room, is piped into the receptive subconscious mind. If the composition is a dirge, its effects are depressing. If it is a spirited allegro composition, its effects are exhilarating.

There are only eight notes in the musical scale. Yet from the variation of these eight notes, thousands of melodies have been written. The amateur who is ignorant of the science of harmonics may combine these notes in clashing, ear-splitting discord. Mental and emotional states of mind are like these basic notes. They can be combined in endless melodies. If the pitch of a person's feelings and emotions form a harmonious melody, a positive consciousness will result. If his thoughts and emotions clash discordantly, the tune he produces will result in a negative frame of mind. Regrettably, many people are amateurs when it comes to the science of mental harmonies and, as a result, produce life-shattering discord.

The route to failure is well-worn by those who have been saying the wrong things to themselves and about themselves. The salesman who has a negative self-appraisal of himself is in effect saying, "Maybe I just don't have what it takes." Or perhaps he rationalizes his failure by placing the blame outside him, saying "I haven't had the breaks; the competition is unfair." At any rate, with his verbal and unverbalized utterances, he can talk his business to death and himself out of a job.

The tragedy of a person's wrong-thinking about himself lies in the fact that he may be cocksure that he is right. The juvenile who flaunts civil authority and feels that laws are for those who are not smart enough to get around them is asking for more trouble than he ever imagines. His attitude attracts others who are talking the same language. Some incident occurs, and the juvenile ends up in court with a delinquency record. In effect, he has talked himself into jail, and, unless his thinking changes, he may talk himself into prison or an untimely death.

A negative self-appraisal need not be as dramatic as

this to bring harm to the personality. A lifetime of dull, monotonous, nonfulfillment may burden the individual with a prison from which the real self eventually must break loose. There is poignant truth in the story of the farm woman who had to be carted off to the mental hospital for treatment. The doctor asked her husband if he had any idea what brought on the derangement. "Can't understand what came over the old woman," the husband replied. "She hain't been out of the kitchen in 20 years."

With the tone of their daily word, people have been talking themselves to death for years. Jeremiah, a sage and prophet of long ago, observed this when he said, "The burden is every man's word." [3] Stated in mental cybernetics terms, man burdens his life with unhappiness, limitation, and failure created by his own negative self-appraisal. By saying the wrong things to himself and about himself, man programs a negative self-image into the creative subconscious. He pipes a discordant, depressing tune into the receptive mind that obeys his thought commands.

## How to monitor the tone of your thinking for self-improvement

As ruler of this wonderful kingdom of yours, you owe it to yourself to monitor carefully the tone of the commands you pipe into the subconscious. Solomon put it well when he said, "Keep thy heart with all diligence, for out of it are the issues of life." [4] If Solomon had spoken in the idiom of today, he might have said, "Monitor the thought images fed into the subconscious with all diligence, for its output will be your experiences in life."

Guard the input! Keep your self-appraisal constructive. Don't lose your temper. Cultivate patience and a bigness toward the mistakes of others. Don't condemn yourself. Monitor the input others would feed into the heart of your feelings and reject the false and undesirable. Turn discouragement aside. Keep yourself busy with self-improvement. Give your attention to your aspirations and goals. Yes, guard the input with all diligence, for from it the subconscious mind issues the experiences of life.

As wise as this advice is, there are two difficulties that may hinder a person in following it:

First, he may not realize that his experiences of limitation, unhappiness, and ineffectiveness are caused by a wrong programming of the mind with false and undesirable data.

Second, even when a person realizes that his tone-of-consciousness is off key, he may have difficulty finding an effective method for building a consciousness that will impel his life toward worthwhile experiences.

### How your consciousness broadcasts

Basic to mental cybernetics is the understanding that new experiences depend upon a change in an individual's self-image—in that composite image produced by his thought and belief. This composite consciousness has its own tonal quality. It has its own wave length. In its reception or sensitivity, the subconscious mind is limited to the wave length on which the conscious mind broadcasts. If day after day a person continues to broadcast on the same frequency of awareness, outer conditions cannot change.

If he entertains thoughts of resentment, self-depreciation, fear, or failure, then negative experiences to match the tonal quality of these states of mind must appear. However, if he guards his thoughts and keeps them tuned to the higher frequencies of love, self-worth, and understanding, his experiences will be positive. To make a switch from negative to positive, a person must change the wave length of his consciousness. He must pay court to the highest ideas and ideals of which he is capable. He must avoid the contamination of hatred and pessimism around him. He must tune out the jarring vibrations of impatience, jealousy, gossip, bickering, worry, and emotional outbursts that burden the heart with unhappiness.

Once the wave length of consciousness is changed and tuned to the positive, the static of undesirable experiences can seldom break into the broadcast. Others of like consciousness are attracted into a person's world and add to his high consciousness. As long as the quality of an individual's mental tone remains high and his thought-dial is on center, the wrong-thinking of others and destructive elements in the mass consciousness around him will find little or no reception.

## INITIAL STEPS TO TAKE

To take the initial step in switching from negative to positive and resetting the wave length of consciousness, you must meet and overcome the two difficulties mentioned above:

First, you must realize that undesirable experiences in your life have been caused by wrong programming of the mind with false, unwise, or inadequate data. The beginning of wisdom is to search the self. Here is where John started, and here is where you must begin. Examine the images lining the darkroom of the subconscious and discover where these images fall short of the wonderful, unique person you really are. Like a picture that lies latent on film awaiting development, the real you is latent and is waiting to be developed. Upon that undeveloped real self, you have superimposed false images that do not do you justice. These false images must be detected to be eliminated.

Second, you must use an effective method to build a new consciousness of the real you. This will require actual change. It will require a daily effort to replace the images that fall short of the ideal with new images that accurately capture the unique, purposeful, wondrous, beautifully designed individual which life has brought forth as you. The mental data processing cards provided in this book will help you in this daily reprogramming of the subconscious. The cards deal with cause. And remember, it is in the realm of mental cause that you must do most of the work to change your life. A law of cause and effect governs all creation. To create anew, you must initiate new causes from which new effects will flow.

## How to set your mental controls

A *daily* effort at change must be made, for, in all likelihood, the old tune you have been playing is a stubborn one. The subconscious has been conditioned or "set" by years of programming to respond automatically. Your mind is very much like an airplane with the "I" of conscious awareness as the pilot. You, the pilot, have the privilege of soaring to a desired height and directing the plane to its destination, after which you may set the craft on automatic control. Unfortunately, you may not have been aware of this privilege and possibly have set your mind on automatic control before climbing to a satisfactory height or before selecting a desirable destination. Perhaps you have been merely skimming the treetops and low-lying hills of mediocre success.

With the use of the laws of mental cybernetics, through conscious control, you can take your mind off automatic *set* and direct your life toward desirable goals. The mind can soar as high in terms of accomplishment as it is programmed to soar. It need not continue to skim the treetops of inadequacy or limitation. But to climb above your present height to new levels of success and fulfillment, you must stop gliding along on easy automatic control and take active steps each day to raise your sights.

Your subconscious mind has become a programmed mechanism. If it is set too low, it is up to you to raise it. It is programmed like the thermostat mentioned in Chapter I. When set at a certain temperature, the mechanism in a thermostat permits the furnace to bring the warmth of the room up to the degree indicated on the thermometer. Then it shuts off automatically and goes no higher. Its regulatory action keeps every room of the house at a fairly constant temperature.

Your self-image is your mental thermostat. It automatically regulates the degree of success to which you may climb and then it shuts off. Its action extends to every room of your mental house, affecting the level of your happiness, business success, companionship and love, and even your health.

If something seems to be holding you back, if you are not demonstrating the extra financial freedom or the personal appreciation and love that would make life complete, examine your mental thermostat. The gauge on your self-image thermometer may be set entirely too low—possibly at a chilly 55 or 60 degrees when 70 or 75 would bring greater comfort. To raise the temperature, you must make a switch from negative to positive. A negative self-image is cold and uninviting. It blocks success, and potential friends find you withdrawn and unapproachable. A positive self-concept makes you radiant and friendly. It attracts success and draws friendship and happiness into your life.

## HOW TO RAISE YOUR SELF-IMAGE THERMOSTAT

Take the steps necessary to turn up the thermostat of your self-image now:

1. Stand before a mirror and practice smiling. Ask yourself if you would respond warmly to such a smile. Keep practicing until your answer is yes.
2. Look deeply into your eyes reflected in the mirror and greet that unique, special, wonderful, beautifully designed self that you really are. Let that self shine forth as you go about your daily tasks.
3. Close your eyes and mentally see yourself surrounded by smiling, pleasant people. Make this the first thing you do in the morning and the last thing you do before going to sleep.
4. Show a genuine interest in other people and in what they do.
5. Develop the habit of looking for ways to compliment others, and sprinkle your language lavishly with "thank you's."
6. Use Mental Data Processing Card No. 4 daily to raise your mental thermostat.

Each day I behold the universe around me and find it friendly. Each day I greet the radiant, successful, considerate, and friendly person that I really am. A positive radiance shines forth through my smile and through my genuine regard for others. A new inner warmth draws to me unprecedented happiness and success.

*Mental Data Processing Card No. 4*

# CHAPTER SUMMARY OF POINTS TO PONDER

1. Daily, you program your mind with the sense data of experience.

2. With this data from your mind and the minds of others, you build your self-image—a composite of thoughts, beliefs, attitudes, and self-evaluations.

3. The conscious mind is like a camera with which you snap impressions of life. The subconscious mind is the darkroom where these pictures are developed.

4. You owe it to yourself to turn the camera of mind upon a self capable of commanding your love. The person who dislikes his self-image projects this dislike upon the world about him.

5. To find this self that is worthy of highest regard, you must become aware of the uniqueness of yourself—the distinct and radiant facet of life that you are.

6. Your mental faculties may be likened to a king and his realm. The throne room of your life is the conscious mind, and the scepter of power resides in your thought and belief. The servant of your mental kingdom is the subconscious mind.

7. As ruler of your mental kingdom, you are always affirming some state of being for yourself. Your word-of-consciousness is the directive power.

8. The tone of your thinking vibrates on a frequency of mind that establishes rapport with others of similar mental set.

9. The automatic "set" of the mind determines the height to which the individual may soar.

10. With the use of the laws of mental cybernetics, through conscious control, you can take your mind off automatic "set" and direct your life toward constructive goals.

# CHAPTER THREE

## How to Monitor Your
## Achievement Program

"Where does experience take place?" I asked the young lady who had paused to brush away a tear with an already dampened tissue. "Does experience happen in time—at some spot on the clock? Or at some spot on the map such as Denver or Chicago? Or does it take place in mind?"

Janet had had an interesting life. She had traveled extensively. She was well-educated. Her home life had been quite ideal. While in college, she met and fell in love with a classmate—a young man whose desire for travel and for the good things of life seemed to parallel her own. Their backgrounds were similar and the marriage appeared ideal. And so it was for over ten years.

But now Janet's world had collapsed. Her husband had fallen in love with another woman. For the moment, my visitor could concentrate on nothing but a tearful recounting of the experiences she and her husband had had together, the trips they had taken, the events of ten years of marriage.

Her whole discourse revealed the one conclusion in her mind—her wonderful experiences were now gone; her life of happiness had come to an end. Probing for a thought that would reverse her conclusion, I asked Janet this question, "Where does experience take place? Where did these events you've been telling me about really happen?"

"As I have told you," she replied, "they happened in many places—Mexico, Miami, New York City—many places."

49

"But," I countered, "there is one locale where all those experiences happened. Where is that place?" I could see that she realized now that I was talking about the room of her own personal awareness. Experience takes place in consciousness!

## Events happen in consciousness

I said to Janet, "You are a young woman. You have had thrilling experiences, possibly more than many people have in a lifetime. I am not going to suggest that you forget the wonderful times you and your husband had together. Let the joy of those memories remain a part of you. However, more experiences are in store for you! Future events will be as marvelous as anything that has happened in the past. Tomorrow's experiences, of course, will happen in the same place where all of your other experiences have occurred. They will take place in your personal awareness—in your consciousness."

"But," Janet objected, "I have no prospects for the future. I may never get married again."

"Whether you marry again or not," I assured her, "your prospects for the future are radiant. You're well-educated. An appreciation of art and beauty is part of your culture. You've always loved to travel, and that love is part of the real you. These qualities belong to the real inner self. They are not shallow, surface qualities that you acquired simply because you were married to someone who loved to travel. Therefore, these qualities are permanent and enduring. They belong to the real self and cannot be lost. Thus, Janet, nothing is really gone. The sense of adventure you have will draw to you the type of experiences you have always loved."

"You see," I explained to the young woman sitting across from me, "your consciousness requires the experiences that belong to it. Actually, events are in mind before they are in the world of affairs. Experiences occur in the outer world as projections of an inner level of awareness."

"Well," Janet broke in, "I know one thing that's really gone. We divided the furniture, and the apartment we decorated together is just an empty memory now."

"Of course," I replied, "there will be things that belonged to your acquired self, the self built during your years as a marriage partner, that will not endure now that you are single. Couples with whom you made friends when you were married may not be as close now, for you are not on the couple circuit anymore. But the worthwhile things that belong to your real self—the deeper level below the mere acquired self—these things will persist in your life and cannot be lost."

### Circumstances and mental cybernetics

The use of mental cybernetics requires the admission that somehow, some way, the experiences in a person's life belong to him. For as long as an individual feels that he had no part to play in the circumstances of his life, he will not know how to take part in changing them.

What are circumstances? What control does man have over them? For the answer, consider the word itself. *Circumstances* comes from the Latin *circum* meaning "around about," plus *stare* meaning "to stand." Simply defined, then, circumstances are "things standing around." The circumstances of your life are those "things standing around you." It is tempting to grant circumstances a life independent of their creator and divorce man from the events he creates. But actually, events have no life independent of the thought power that is the cause of their "standing around."

What about the circumstances and events in your life? Are you responsible for the "things standing around"? Before you answer, consider this analogy: Imagine that you have moved into a new house or apartment. Assuming that you did the packing yourself, the glassware, linens, and dozens of household items were temporarily packed in boxes and barrels. These various and assorted containers hold your worldly possessions. These crates and cartons you packed are now "standing around you." Think of the circumstances of your life as the crates and barrels that you have packed through the years. They contain what you put in them. Now they are standing around you.

Even if other people helped you pack, it was you who

permitted them to fill the boxes that are now piled around you. The boxes are stuffed with mental images, impressions, attitudes, preferences, set reactions, and prejudices. If some of the contents are undesirable and you failed to screen the mental data packaged for you, then you are due for some unpleasant surprises when you unpack. The output will be governed by the input.

The output from all the mental and emotional data fed into your inner computer becomes the events, conditions, and experiences standing around you. Some of that data derives from the real you, some belongs to your acquired self (as was the case with Janet's acquired status as a married person), and some derives from other people whose lives affect yours. In addition to parents, spouses, close relatives, teachers, religious counselors, and business associates, people you have never met may have done a major job of packing your life with circumstances. For example, the data that pours into your mind from the actions of legislators, lobbyists, editors, and newscasters affects what takes place in your consciousness. There is an intimate relationship between the influences of others and the things you see standing around you as circumstances.

## IMPORTANCE OF CAUSATIVE FACTORS

It is vitally important to realize the causative factors by which things come into being. It is *more* important to understand how you can create other circumstances— how you can do a better job of packing than the one that has been done. Although it is true that the contents of the barrels surrounding you may have been derived from a shallow, acquired self or from others who helped you pack, the point is that you do not have to let indiscriminate influences program your consciousness. It is your privilege to screen the mental data that would be packaged and placed around you as circumstances. It is your responsibility to monitor the program that is fed into the creative subconscious mind and to reject negative data.

In Chapter I you learned that man is much like a

computer programmer whose duty it is to plan a logical, rational, and purposeful program. He must know the industry this program is to serve and what the output is to achieve. You have the same responsibility in regard to the marvelous subconscious computer within you. You must have a total plan for yourself that is logical and purposeful. You must know the goals which this total program is to serve and what achievements you wish to demonstrate. Then, you must consciously screen the sense-data that comes to you daily and utilize only that which conforms to your achievement program. The conscious mind must learn how to serve you as your achievement program monitor. When it does, you will have control over the influences you package and keep as the circumstances surrounding you.

### How to use awareness and attention to monitor your program

Horace Mann once said, "Superiority to circumstances is one of the most prominent characteristics of great men." The science of mental cybernetics affirms that all men are great for they have the latent ability to demonstrate control over circumstances through the use of the greater mind of which they are individualized expressions. To demonstrate control over circumstances in your personal world, use the techniques suggested in the five steps that follow:

**1.** Recognize clearly that conditions are not things of themselves. They do not have an independent life of their own apart from their creator. They are like the crates and cartons filled with bric-a-brac standing around. The quality of that accumulated bric-a-brac may be impeccable. It may be mediocre. Or it may be a collection of odds and ends. At any rate, the quality of the thought content of his mind is that with which man builds his environment, his success or failure. This thought content is the blueprint by which he builds his palace or his hut.

**2.** Accept this basic premise of mental cybernetics: *Circumstances are packaged thoughts.* Because you packaged them in the first place, you have the privilege of repacking them. Hence, circumstances and present conditions are not unalterable. It may be true that others have helped you load your mind with beliefs, ideas, attitudes, prejudices, and conditioned responses. But, just because present circumstances are packed in a certain way, you are not forced to keep them unaltered. You do not need to acquiesce to conditions that are producing undesirable results. You do need, however, to take the initiative in repacking the thought content of your mind in such a way that new, desirable conditions and experiences will result.

**3.** Realize that the sides of the boxes that hold the circumstances surrounding you are built of attention. The wooden barrel staves that keep your thought content intact are hewn of attention. Attention, primarily, is the thing that gives support to the images, attitudes, habit reactions, and behavior patterns packed and piled around you now. Conditions as you see them cannot and will not stand around without support. That support may be both conscious and unconscious. It may be negative or positive. All too often, through his irritation with unsatisfactory circumstances, man gives his attention to negative conditions without realizing it. Through impatience, criticism, disgust, griping, and self-pity, man can intensify with attention the very negative conditions of his life that he deplores. Unintentionally, he may be holding undesirable conditions to him with the power of attention.

**4.** Resolve that you will use the power of your attention as a device to demonstrate new circumstances. Let old undesirable conditions dissolve by withdrawing your attention from them. Let the sides of the box containing them fall away. Attend to other qualities that will create new circumstances. Many conditions exist simply because a person has not attended to positive concepts and attitudes. One's life may be filled with unhappiness, with a feeling of inferiority, with poverty, or with a sour disposition, but, by giving attention to positive qualities of thought, one will encourage desirable conditions to manifest.

**5.** Organize the circumstances you would like to see

54

standing around you into a definite design. Envision well-ordered, pleasant surroundings. Include the success you want to demonstrate and the goals to which you aspire. Visualize yourself in the environment that would make you happy. This design is your *achievement program.* Now, give your attention to this program daily. Be consciously attentive to feelings, actions, and mental images that enhance that plan. But, just as important, be aware of doubts and self-depreciation that are foreign to the plan and refuse to entertain them. Use your conscious attention to monitor your daily thought content and keep it geared to the design you have planned for your life. "Keep thy heart with all diligence, for out of it are the issues of life."

### How to fulfill the universal script

The ability to demonstrate "superiority to circumstances" comes with a realization that the universal scheme of things is vaster by far than the tiny segment man sees around him. Man is much like a playgoer who enters the theater after the curtain has gone up. This confused member of the audience has no knowledge of the beginning of the story and no conception of what the ending may be. The script does not make sense and he wonders what's going on. Similarly, in the drama of life, many of the playgoers live out their lives without a clear understanding of the plot. The script seems pointless and confused, and they fail to grasp the grand scope of the universal drama in which they are participating.

What is the scope of the universal drama? Into its script has been written a vital role for each man. It speaks of wisdom, personal success, creative expression, the satisfaction of service to others, and self-fulfillment for each actor. It speaks of a power for each man, based on the ingenuity of mind that makes him superior to seemingly impossible conditions. "If you have faith as a grain of mustard seed, you shall say to this mountain [whatever your personal mountain may be—disappointment, lack of achievement, guilt, loneliness, dissatisfaction] be thou removed and cast into yonder sea, and it shall be done; and nothing shall be impossible to you."

Things appear impossible and conditions seem insurmountable only when man's vision is focused on an isolated segment of the universal drama. He enters after the curtain has gone up. He is ignorant of the beginning of the story and apprehensive of the end. Problems of the present loom up as threats and are out of proportion with the whole. Thus, the script is distorted. To man it may appear that the script calls for failure when in the grand sweep of things it requires success. He may feel that the musical score calls for a dirge when the total composition is a song of love and life. He may bind himself with chains of false circumstances in the midst of freedom. He may loiter in unproductivity when the script calls for creativity.

This does not mean that there are not those who play their parts in life well. There are some who sense the purposefulness of the script and fill their roles masterfully. Regrettably, there are others who are ignorant of their potentialities and resign themselves to limitation. Perhaps they remark, "Oh, I accept my lot without complaining." If a person feels he must be content with an unhappy or restricted role, he has misread the universal script. Each role expands to infinite proportions when viewed from the scope of the entire drama. Each man's role is vital. It is essential. In fact, there are no bit players in the universal scheme. There are none whose lowly role is simply to serve as a background for the stars. Each man—with his unique, special, original, and individually evolved qualities—is like a guest star in a television spectacular. The guest stars, no matter how many of them may appear, all have a unique worth to add to the production.

You are here to find and fill the guest-star role for which you are destined in the script of the universal drama. You are here to read the script correctly and become aware that you have unique qualities and gifts to give mankind that no one else can contribute. These unique qualities will carry you to stardom. They will carry you to success and fulfillment as you give unstintingly of the special person you really are.

Now, using the techniques outlined in the five steps listed in this chapter, design an achievement program for yourself. Write it down, if you wish, or think it through until it is well-defined and real. Put into it a recognition of your unique value and your claim to greatness as one of the guest stars in the universal drama. Remember the wisdom, power, success, and creative contribution to mankind that is written into the script for you. Then use the device of your attention to keep your daily mental input geared to this achievement program. Refresh your attention as programmer twice each day for a week by reading Mental Data Processing Card No. 5.

I am superior to circumstance for I possess the thought power with which circumstances are made. With that power, I now design an achievement program that carries me to fulfillment in a role vital to the universal drama. With that power, I monitor the mental and emotional data pouring in each day. I reject that which is foreign to the design. I utilize that which enhances and advances my achievement program.

*Mental Data Processing Card No. 5*

## How the acquired self differs from the real self

In the process of living his life in unison with others, man forms what mental cybernetics calls the acquired self. Man, through his perception of the attitudes, beliefs, and conditions of his environment, identifies quite unconsciously with the atmosphere around him. Unwittingly, his environmental identification may be with financial freedom or its lack. It may be with happiness or its absence. It may be with love or loneliness. Influenced by these factors, man builds up an image of himself in the subconscious level of mind. This image becomes stronger and stronger and reaches the point where its influence is the dominant theme of his personality. This image is man's acquired self.

How does the acquired self differ from the real self? The real self is the genuine you. It is one of life's special guest stars. Its potentialities have barely been scratched; its latent wisdom awaits development; its grandeur has scarcely been tapped. Obscuring that real self is the acquired self you have been working on since birth. Starting at a tender age, you begin to acquire self-identification as a member of a home, community, religious group, and social level. A self emerged from the many impressions and images you acquired from the rich, poor, or middle-class atmosphere in which you were reared. This self emerged naturally and normally through conditioning, imitation, training, and the desire to belong. This acquired self may be negative or positive, but in any event, it does not match the full power and mastery that is potential to the real self.

There may be many facets to this acquired self or assembly-of-selves. The average person is called upon to play many roles. A woman, for example, may have children who cast her into a mother's role at home. She may have a career that demands her performance as a business woman at work. For her husband she plays the part of a wife, and for her mother she performs as a daughter. She has built an image of her status in each one of the roles she plays. These acquired images may crowd out the real self, the self of latent grandeur that needs recognition, respect, creative expression, and self-fulfillment simply as an individual.

**What self acts as stand-in for you?**

The acquired self is something like a stand-in groomed to take the place of a star at certain places in the production. For example, a woman acting as stand-in for one of the top feminine stars will be about the same height and weight and have similar coloring. She will stand under the hot flood lights for testing, while the leading lady remains comfortable, cool, and rested. If the stand-in is a stunt woman hired to perform a special skill or a dangerous feat, her hair will be styled like the star's, her clothes will be identical with those of the star, and she will be groomed to walk and gesture like the leading lady. She does not possess the full power and mastery of the star, but the temporary illusion fools the audience—and perhaps the star as well.

As one of life's special guest stars, you may be fooled by the selves that stand in for you—those acquired, surface selves that do not represent your full potentialities and power. Stop and consider for a moment how many stand-ins or representatives you may have. Count the different facets of your personality that may have developed through identifying with various people or with various factors in your environment. There will probably be a number, for few people have achieved a unity with the real self. For example, in regard to finances, there may be a facet of your personality that cringes each month-end when the bills pour in. If so, your stand-in has identified with a fear of limitation and lack. In regard to your social life, there may be a facet of your personality that feels unloved or inferior. If so, your stand-in has identified too long with self-depreciation. Examine your life now and find out what self is acting as stand-in for you.

Then, don't be fooled into thinking that you are the stand-in. Remember, in addition to the fact that a stand-in does the less-desirable, tiresome jobs, he also receives less pay than the star commands. Why let your stand-in support you when you have the potentialities and the power of the guest star himself?

### How to determine your core concept

Each expression of yourself that you acquire, each stand-in, brings experiences to you that conform to its role. If you are a champion of causes, that self may say "I will not rest until I see justice done." If you are a born critic, that self may declare, "I tell it as it is regardless of how it hurts." Each expression of "I" will draw to it reactions that correspond. Each expression of "I" becomes causative of experience. Of course, the self with which you identify most often becomes dominant. This dominant image serves as the *core concept* that gives birth to the majority of experiences that take place in your consciousness.

Around this core concept man's life revolves. It is the hub to which his total thinking tends to conform. For example, if a person's core concept is one of unworthiness, all of his thinking will be tainted by this belief. In his relationships with others, he will find experiences that validate his belief. In his home, in his place of employment, and in his social contacts, he will unconsciously communicate his feeling of unworthiness to others who will react in ways that confirm the impression he has imparted.

Or consider the person who has created what could be called a critic-image. This person sees flaws in everyone and everything. He is the chronic critic who could set the world right if those around him would just follow his advice.

## CASE HISTORY OF A CRITIC IMAGE

I remember the first time I met a young man named Ed. I was associated with an industry at the time, and Ed was hired to work in my department. When the foreman introduced Ed to me, I was impressed by his air of vitality and enthusiasm. He seemed to be the type that would go right to the top in any line of work he wanted to do.

Before long, however, I noted that this young man seemed unduly critical of how things were being run. The foreman was not as brilliant as Ed felt a foreman should be. Even the superintendent came in for a barrage of criticism because of certain decisions Ed felt were wrong.

Ed attracted to himself others who were inclined to be critical of the policies of the company. Very soon a negative atmosphere pervaded the whole department. One morning Ed did not show up for work. It turned out that he had been called to the office the evening before and given the opportunity to seek employment elsewhere.

The Eds of the world who harbor things-are-being-done-wrong concepts pick away on the decisions and policies of others. "The boss is incompetent," they complain. "How did such a jerk of a foreman ever reach that position?" This critic-image or core concept begins to attract others with a budding critic-image. The Eds become a clearing house for other malcontents. Soon they radiate a negative aura that alienates those who are the object of the criticism. An unwelcome visit to the head office for the traditional pink slip comes next.

What about Ed? Did losing his job cause him to wise up? Probably not. More than likely, he carried his critic-image to his next job and soon found justification for new complaints. The irony is that Ed felt entirely righteous. His stand-in self was performing its role superbly as a critic. If his negative approach caused him to lose one job after another, his stand-in knew how to blame others for his failure. Yes, other people did not appreciate the brilliancy of his mind. They were jealous. They were shortsighted and short on judgment. And his stand-in self found ample proof to reinforce his core belief. Ed's real problem was having allowed his stand-in "critic" self to become so dominant in the first place.

### How to control your mental data input

Why does man permit himself to be conditioned to core concepts that are detrimental? How does he acquire a domineering critic-image or an inferiority complex or a colorless personality image or a poverty complex or accident proneness? How does he establish in his subconscious mind these patterns that repeat themselves with monotonous regularity?

By means of the data input valve of conscious awareness, man absorbs impressions, imbibes unscreened mental data, and merges with the thought forces surrounding him. In the process, he identifies with various opinions and impressions about him that emerge as his self-image. That image may represent him as friendly or withdrawn. It may depict him as confident or unsure. It may present him as a celebrity or a nonentity. It all depends on whether the conscious input valve was open wide to indiscriminate data or whether man monitored the input wisely. Remember, it is necessary to give conscious attention to screening the data that pour into the mind each day. Half-truths about the self, remarks that are belittling, criticism that is unjustified, and insinuations that are unwarranted must be blocked with conscious monitoring and turned aside before they warp the self-image.

A distorted self-image can be acquired so easily when the input valve of conscious awareness is left unguarded that a man sometimes feels, "It's just my nature to be this way." He thinks, "I'm *naturally* shy and uncomfortable with strangers," or "I'm *naturally* a loud talker and the life of the party." He may indeed be either way, but not *naturally*. He may be that way from the standpoint of programming but not from the standpoint of nature. The self he calls "natural" is acquired through a complex process of conditioning.

Indeed, it might be more realistic for a person to say, "I'm artificially shy and uncomfortable with strangers," for he has acquired a pattern that is not natural to the real self. He is playing a role that has been built up mechanically or artificially through conditioning.

Many years ago scientists demonstrated how animals react to conditioning in the establishment of artificial patterns of behavior. The science of mental cybernetics reveals how man reacts to conditioning in the establishment of self-image patterns. The classic example of conditioning was the experiment conducted by Pavlov with a dog. Each time food was placed before the dog, a bell was rung. The dog soon came to associate the bell with dinner time and salivated when food was placed before him. In time, Pavlov's dog would salivate whenever the bell was rung without even smelling food. He did not salivate naturally at the ringing of a bell. He salivated *naturally* at the smell of food and *artificially* at the ringing of the bell.

In like manner, man has become conditioned to the ringing of bells. The bell of criticism rings and man reacts with pangs of self-depreciation or with hostility. The bell of prejudice rings and man reacts with irrational violence. These reactions are artificial. They do not belong to the real self, but they have been acquired through conditioning and through a conscious mind that was open wide to indiscriminate thought forces around it.

Examine yourself to determine if you are accepting an artificial, stand-in self as being what you really are. Do you monitor the flow through the input valve of the conscious mind? Do you screen out the negative, or do you say "I" to every mood, to every feeling, to every frustration? Do irritations around you trigger the bell and cause you to say, "I am offended; I have been insulted; I have been hurt; I am depressed; I am a failure"? If so, you are conditioned to artificial reactions that are not worthy of or natural to the real you.

## The importance of screening of mental data

In the technological field of cybernetics, a vital function is the screening of the data to be used in computer programming. The purpose of data screening is to detect errors and omissions in coding that would result in mistakes in later analyses. Screening also reveals inaccurately keypunched data or cards that have been folded, stapled, or mutilated, which would produce erroneous results. The accuracy of the information fed into the computer is vital to correct results. The input determines the output.

In the personal field of mental cybernetics, data screening or monitoring is just as vital. Errors or inaccuracies in perception are like errors in coding. They can lead to mistaken conclusions about the self. Falsely programmed mental data, multiplied by fear, ignorance, self-pity, prejudice, and the like, produce erroneous and even disastrous results in life. Therefore, careful attention must be given to the exercise of daily screening of attitudes, reactions, impressions, and thoughts, for the quality of the data fed into the personal computer of the subconscious determines the results. The mental input determines the experience output.

If there are certain aspects of your life that are unsatisfactory, if the output seems to be something of a sorry scheme, you may feel much like the fabled Omar Khayyam who philosophized:

> Ah, Love! Could you and I with him conspire
> To grasp this sorry scheme of things entire,
> Would not we shatter it to bits—and then,
> Remold it nearer to the heart's desire? [1]

With mental cybernetics, you can indeed remold life closer to the heart's desire. You can conspire with that creative cause within you once you recognize and appreciate your role in the creative process. In Chapter 1 you learned that the role of the conscious mind is to choose and direct, while the role of the subconscious is to obey and create. Therefore, to direct well, you must *consciously* choose and screen your thoughts wisely.

## STEPS IN EFFECTIVE SCREENING

To practice effective data monitoring, you must try to detect and screen out daily thoughts that enhance the acquired self to the exclusion of the real self. Remember Ed? His critic-self was so dominant that he chose daily data that enhanced and advanced only his critic-image. Therefore, in screening your daily thought input, keep these points in mind:

*First,* in the process of living, you have acquired a personality self that is something less than the highest and best of which your real self is capable. You are more than the person you see. Your image in the mirror is evidence of your being but not of the sum total of you. The surface nature of personality is revealed in the root definition of the word. It comes from the Latin *persona,* meaning mask, as worn by actors. Thus, your personality expression is a mask worn by the real self as it performs upon the stage of life. This surface expression acts as stand-in for you.

Just as the stand-in never reaches the full power and mastery of the star or commands the same salary, your surface-personality self does not express the total essence of the real self. Therefore, choose daily thoughts about your potentialities that conform more closely to the person you want to be and screen out images that belong to your lesser stand-in self.

*Second,* to detect erroneous data with which you may be programming your mind, try to catch yourself in the act when something unpleasant happens. Observe your actions and reactions in regard to your work, your environment, and your friends. When external stimuli impinge upon you, how do you react? Do external impressions always ring the same bell and bring an automatic answer, like a taped telephone answering device? If the boss criticizes your work, do you react with a pretaped barrage of hostility? If someone is sarcastic, do you retort with a ready barbed reply? If so, you are reacting with a self that is conditioned to hostility and vindictiveness. Try to catch all reactions that do not belong to the real self and screen them out of your consciousness. In their place cultivate reactions worthy of the real you. Cultivate forgiveness, gratitude, love, harmony, understanding, and a bigness toward mankind.

*Third,* at the close of each day before retiring, examine your behavior by reversing the time track of the day. Start by recalling the most recent events and retrace experiences back to the beginning of the day. In regard to each experience, ask the question: "Did I act or react in the best possible way?" Often the answer will be no. In your imagination, reshoot the event like a movie scene and make the corrections that would have improved the situation. Mentally reshooting unpleasant scenes of the day helps you to: (a) observe the action from a more relaxed, less emotional position, (b) rehearse the role as second thoughts would indicate that it should have been played, (c) break your identification with the situation, and (d) condition your mind so that when a like situation arises on the wheel of recurrence, you will be prepared to play the role to better advantage.

Give daily attention to placing a check on your mental data input valve of conscious awareness. Monitor the

Relaxed and unemotional, I now review the scenes of my day. This scene [identify one] was not worthy of my real self. Mentally reshooting the event, I see myself in full command of my mind. I see myself acting with patience, harmony, love, and a bigness toward others. I forgive myself, vowing never to permit such pettiness to recur. I release the original scene and identify only with the "retake" now filling my mind.

*Mental Data Processing Card No. 6*

intake wisely and no longer will the door to the deeper mind stand open to indiscriminate and unconscious programming. Persist in these steps listed above to detect errors in the perception of events and to channel into the subconscious actions and reactions which will bring forth superior results in your life.

Use Mental Data Processing Card No. 6 to help you reshoot any scenes at the end of the day that were unpleasant or that linger unhappily in your memory.

## CHAPTER SUMMARY OF POINTS TO PONDER

1. Circumstances—as things standing around you—are packed with the thought content of your desires, attitudes, concepts, and beliefs.

2. Others may have helped you pack your life with circumstances, but this does not relieve you of the responsibility of repackaging your mind with thought material that will create new circumstances.

3. Attention is the means whereby you may monitor the thought food that becomes processed as experience and circumstances.

4. In the process of living, you form or acquiesce to the formation of an acquired self which you take to be real.

5. This acquired or conditioned self acts as stand-in for the real you.

6. Those acquired characteristics which become dominant form a core-concept that acts with centripetal force, drawing events and experiences to you.

7. By means of the data input valve of conscious awareness, you can guard the door to the inner kingdom of mind where self-images are stored.

8. Wise data preparation and screening are vital to catch errors in coding sense impressions, to monitor and reject data that does not conform to your achievement program, and to add the magic factors of patience and gratitude.

# CHAPTER
# FOUR

*How to Explore
and Use Inner
Mental Space*

"Three, two, one," the countdown was complete! A technician pushed the remote-control button from the blockhouse, and the giant rocket rose from its pad. In the nose cone seasoned astronauts, veterans of a soft landing on the moon, reclined on their couches. They waited tensely for the second stage to fire. Then it came! With a thrust that seemed to push them into eternity, the second-stage rockets fired, and the ship broke free of the earth's gravity.

As prescheduled, the spent second stage was jettisoned next, along with the nose-cone shield protecting the space capsule. The craft at last was free of the pull of the earth and was in outer space.

The commander spoke, "Correct for any deviation in the takeoff and set the course for Arcturus."

"Yes, sir," came the reply, and the craft hurtled through space on its journey toward one of the nearest neighboring stars 32.6 light years from the sun.

Would the mission succeed? What might the crew of the Arcturus flight find? It is quite reasonable to believe that existing in the unlimited galaxies of space there are different forms of life. One cannot keep faith with reason and at the same time hypothesize that the earth is the only planet where consciousness has come to flower as self-awareness. In the evolutionary unfoldment of life forms, the self-reflective state awakens wherever conditions are right for that awakening. Indeed, there may be planets where consciousness is so highly developed that the degree of awareness man has achieved would be crude by comparison.

Although a trip to Arcturus may belong in the realm of fantasy today, there are no predictable limits to man's curiosity and the distance he may travel in the exploration of outer space. Hardly a day passes without news of scientific breakthroughs relative to man's conquest of space. What man can dream, man can do. And, from walking on the moon to stepping from star to star, is a short distance in the mind of man.

Not too long ago, the moon was an object of adoration for lovers. Now men here on earth have watched by means of television their fellowmen walking on the moon. It's no longer a joke to speculate that in a few years it will be just another parking lot. Man has found in outer space an endless world to explore and conquer. Its boundaries at present seem limitless. Its potentialities stagger the imagination.

The lure of outer space, however, belongs to the skilled astronaut, physicist, and astronomer. More personal and more immediately important is another space realm that is open to every man's exploration—the inner realm of mind. Man is a being of two worlds. His essential beingness exists in a world of consciousness—a world of thought, ideas, and concepts. The second world is that of form and effect—a world of things, appearances, and extensions. In a sense these two worlds are one and the same, like the two sides of the coin mentioned in Chapter One. Form is a conscious concept, while the subconscious mind contains the inherent possibility of *all* form. These two expressions of the one coin-of-mind are equally vast. In both directions they reach out to infinity. No man has reached the heights of conscious awareness, nor has any man probed the depths of subjective potentiality.

## The profitable exploration of inner space

Through the centuries, a few mental explorers have probed great depths of mind. Their reports, when understood, are more exciting than the discoveries that will come from outer space. To explore the possibilities of one's own mind is the greatest of all undertakings and the most profitable of all enterprises. The treasure from the inner kingdom of mind is the greatest wealth that man can possess. It is the cause of all external wealth, whether the treasure be happiness, power, peace of mind, or abundance of supply. Come with me, then, on a journey of exploration into the inner mind—the most profitable of all quests.

### What to do when lost in mental space

Man's speculations about outer space have given rise to many fancies. Science fiction and television have long since placed man in space and depicted his encounters there. One series would have man "lost in space" and wandering among the planets of the universe, trapped one time by a race of robots, tricked by a band of vegetable people another time, and next threatened by a mad scientist likewise lost in space. Space exploration, no doubt, will present certain hazards, but the prospect of being lost in outer space is no more perilous than being lost in mental space.

Man, through little fault of his own, can become lost in the inner space of his own mental kingdom. He may lose his way through disappointment, self-depreciation, and feelings of guilt. He may lose his way through impulsiveness and impatience. His way may become encrusted with a sour, critical, negative disposition. Or, he may be lost simply because he never suspected there was a way to understand himself.

The last statement seems to be true for mankind in general. Young people of the world seem to sense this lack of understanding of the self. They are searching for answers to this age-old problem, and they will not be content with age-old answers. A new direction is necessary. Fresh solutions are desperately needed.

As long as man is lost in mental space, just so long will he be lost in the outer world of form and effect. He is not going to find something better outside of him until he finds something that is superior within. A fundamental law of mental cybernetics is this: *The results that are dem-*

*onstrated in your experience can be no better than the data fed into the mind.* If mankind seems to be lost here in the world of experience—in wars, riots, and frustrations—it is due to the fact that too many people are lost in the inner space of their own minds. If man is lost in mental space, what path may he take to find himself? The science of mental cybernetics can direct man to that path and to the discovery of his real self.

### How to recognize the mental state in which you live

It is a rule of survival along the trail to stop if you are lost. Stop and get your bearings. If you can find a rise, look for familiar landmarks. If the sun is shining, stop and identify the points of the compass. Don't stumble on blindly, but pause and appraise your surroundings. Gather clues as to your present location before attempting another path.

The same rule is a wise one for the person who may not know where he is going in life—for the man who is wandering aimlessly in mental space. He would do well to stop and appraise his present status. He should pause and seek clues regarding his whereabouts in the scheme of things.

A person may be perfectly familiar with his physical whereabouts. He may know well enough the house he lives in, the street on which the house stands, the town in which it is located, and the state in which he resides. However, he may never have considered his mental whereabouts. Mentally, the state in which man resides is that of consciousness. The mental house in which he lives is the thought atmosphere of his mind. The individual decor of his mental house is strictly original, furnished with the uniqueness of his own values, attitudes, preferences, memories, habit patterns, and self-images. Unlike the stationary brick and mortar home in which man lives, his mental house is easily moved with him. It goes wherever he goes.

The street on which man's mental house is located is the route his emotions travel most frequently. That street may easily become a rut that holds man to a monotonous repetition of experiences. It is easy to fall into the habit of frequenting certain places. When you leave your house in the morning, more than likely you take the same route to work. Over and over you shop at the same supermarket, patronize the same barber shop or beauty parlor, stop at the same familiar bistro, and do business with the same clothing store.

It is easy, too, to fall into the habit of frequenting certain states of being. Something triggers your emotions, and your response carries you down the familiar route of antagonism or hostility. Something stirs your memory, and down to the old harbor of resentment you go, perhaps taking a turn around the swamp of despair or the bog of frustration. Year after year you may find yourself frequenting the same attitudes, feelings, and desires. This is the place where you live—in your mental house located on the street your emotions travel most often.

Do you like the place where you live now? Pause and appraise your present status. What do you like and dislike regarding your whereabouts? This you must know before you can decide where you want to go in life. This you must know before you can change the state of consciousness in which you reside.

If the same experiences keep happening to you year after year, it is due to the fact that you are traveling the same streets of thought, attitude, and belief. The same street will lead to the same scenery. This is also true of friendships. Just as you have certain neighbors because of the location of the lots on which your brick and mortar house stands, so you will have certain neighbors because of where you live in your mind. You will have an affinity for those who live on the same mental street as you. The ideas, attitudes, and desires that you frequent draw to you both friends and experiences of a like nature.

WHERE HAVE YOUR THOUGHT PATHS LED YOU?

As you pause to get your bearings before attempting a new path, you may be surprised at where you find yourself. There are as many mental states and variations in consciousness as there are places on the map. There is the sophisticated New York City state of mind, thrifty

71

rural Pennsylvania mental state, the bustling Los Angeles consciousness, the rustic Ozark state of mind, and so on. The ways in which "inner space" has been individualized are endless, for man lives in a state of consciousness of his own unique creation. Each person is like an inner city unto himself with its crisscross of streets laid out by the many thought paths his mind has taken through the years. And where have those thought paths led? To an elite address in Paradise Hills or to poverty row?

If your own inner city of mind could be mapped, would the diagram look like the one in Figure 4–1? This diagram is a typical mapping of the paths of consciousness. Pick out the street on which you live in the interior city of your mind. Do you live on the Road of Hope that leads to the Hill of Happiness and the Pinnacle of Peace? Are you on your way to success and creative fulfillment symbolized by a Paradise Hills consciousness? Do you drive home along the Highway of Health that leads to vitality and vigor?

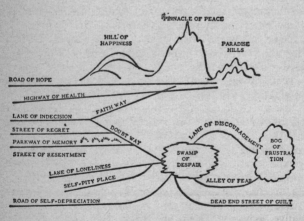

*Figure 4–1*

When circumstances force you onto the Lane of Indecision, do you take Faith Way, the fork that leads upward, or do you make a wrong turn downward onto Doubt Way? Because of the mistakes you have made,

72

do you tend to live on the Street of Regret which inter-
sects with Doubt Way and leads down to the Swamp
of Despair and the Bog of Frustration?

The Streets of Regret and Resentment form a double
lane of negative thinking running along the Parkway of
Memory. Memory plays a major role in reinforcing the
thought paths of resentment and regret. What is the
dominant tone of your memory? Do you permit the
unhappy experience of yesterday to dictate to you
today? Do you allow the slights, hurts, and humiliations
you have experienced in the past to possess your mind
now while the many favors and kind acts rendered to
you fade from recall? This was the case with Alice.

## CASE HISTORY OF A NEGATIVE MEMORY

Alice Z. had a wonderful memory. She remembered
everything from A to Z, but it was all of a negative
nature. I remember the first time I met Alice. She came
to my office and began to pour forth a steady stream
of criticism about her marriage partner. She complained
of how badly her husband had treated her and how he
grabbed her arm and bruised it. Motioning to an area
of her upper arm, she explained in detail how discolored
it had turned. As she spoke of her husband's cruelty,
she recalled that her mother had warned her that she
was making a big mistake when she married.

I tried to remain objective in order to discover both
sides of the problem, but I soon found myself agreeing
that Alice must be justified in her accusations. Then
something she said made me realize that she was recounting experiences from out of a distant past. The husband
who had been the big mistake of her life had long since
been divorced and was now married to another woman.

Alice's real mistake was not her marriage but her
negative memory. Daily she took the double lanes of
Resentment and Regret running along the Parkway of
Memory and found herself circling the Swamp of Despair
year after year.

There is not a person who has not made mistakes in
judgment. Everyone does things that later he finds he
should not have done. But the greatest mistake of all is

that of reliving mistakes mentally—traversing the same streets of regret, frustration, and resentment day after day, year after year.

## How to furnish your house of mind

Plot your present mental whereabouts on the diagram in Figure 4-1. Pick out the mental street on which you have built your house of consciousness. If the surroundings are not constructive, if you tend to dwell on paths located on the lower portion of the map, it is your prerogative to move. Take yourself up the Road of Hope. Build a new mental house with new furnishings on the Hill of Happiness or the Pinnacle of Peace.

Emerson spoke of this prerogative, this privilege you have to build a superior dwelling in inner space, when he wrote:

> Every spirit builds itself a house, and beyond its house a world, and beyond its world a heaven. Know then that the world exists for you. . . . What we are, that only can we see. All that Adam had, all that Caesar could, you have and can do. Adam called his house heaven and earth. Caesar called his house Rome; you perhaps call yours a cobbler's trade; a hundred acres of plowed land; or a scholar's garret. Yet line for line and point for point, your dominion is as great as theirs, though without fine names. Build therefore your own world. As fast as you conform your life to the pure idea in your mind, *that* will unfold its great proportions.[1]

Build for yourself a heaven on earth, a heaven in consciousness. Furnish your new home with the thought-decor that will make for comfortable living. Hang the walls of your home with constructive images of the person you aspire to be. Like colors, thoughts have their hues. Keep your thoughts harmonious and complimentary. Attitudes that conflict are like colors that clash. Their discordant effect makes you restless and irritable.

The furniture you bring into your mental dwelling—the beliefs, desires, and aspirations—should be in good taste. The furniture you choose for your own mental home must never rob another of his possessions. Your desires must be unselfish and a blessing not only to you but to all concerned.

And what about the music of your mind, the symphony of thoughts piped to every room throughout the day? Keep the fidelity high with the best moods of which you are capable. Choose not a dirge of resentment or self-recrimination. Select an album of constructive mood-music to brighten your day.

As Emerson pointed out, "All that Adam had, all that Caesar could, you have and can do." [2] This is true, but as yet few people have demonstrated the potentialities of such affluence. Mankind is very much like a city full of people whose homes are spacious and beautiful. The main floors of the houses are luxuriously furnished with the finest brocades, richly grained woods, and priceless tapestries. Sunlight streams through the main floor windows and reveals an interior intended for gracious living. But where are the tenants of these houses to be found? The majority are existing in the darkened basements, unaware of the upstairs that stands empty and unutilized, awaiting their discovery.

How foolish it would be for the owner of a lovely mansion of many rooms to spend his days in the gloom of the servants' quarters. Yet you may be doing just that. You may be conforming to a mental rut that confines you to a monotonous day spent going from cramped quarters to the kitchen, the pantry, and back again. You may be spending your day in the basement of consciousness with the upper rooms of attainment and self-fulfillment boarded up.

However, as Emerson wrote, "As fast as you conform your life to the pure idea in your mind, *that* will unfold its great proportions." [3] The greater proportions of the mental house in which you dwell, those unused upper rooms of consciousness, will unfold as you become aware of them. You have already been given a mansion, a dwelling of many rooms, represented by the innumerable mental abilities, capacities, and talents potential to you.

You, however, must open the doors to those rooms. This you do by expanding your awareness of the real self; by putting faith in your ability to perform and produce at a higher level; by designing a mental world that is superior in decor to your present surroundings. A new poise, power, skill, and mastery will show itself when you conform your consciousness to the pure nature of the real self. With this self, build yourself a house. Build yourself a heaven.

Choose now the mental street on which you will live, steering clear of the Lane of Loneliness and Self-Pity Place. Vacate the basement of consciousness for the upper rooms of attainment and self-fulfillment. Discard mental furnishings of prejudice, criticism, and envy. Choose instead the rich brocades of generosity, patience, service to others, optimism, and love. The decor of your new mental home awaits your designing hand.

Avoid the clutter of many petty desires. Design your mental home around one central theme of self-improvement and self-mastery—and all the rest that belongs to the kingdom will be added unto you. Choose that theme now and work to conform your thoughts, responses, plans, and actions to it. Use Mental Data Processing Card No. 7 for one week, reading it in the morning and evening, to help you make a mental house of beauty and power.

> Out of the stuff of thought I now build a new consciousness in which to dwell. I choose the street wisely by controlling the emotion-paths my mind traverses daily. I keep the decor uncluttered by disciplining my desires to one dominant theme of power and beauty. My new consciousness blesses me and all who dwell near me in mind.

*Mental Data Processing Card No. 7*

> "Every one that heareth these sayings of
> mine, and doeth them not, shall be likened unto
> a foolish man, which built his house upon the
> sand: And the rain descended, and the floods
> came, and the winds blew, and beat upon that
> house; and it fell: and great was the fall of it." [4]

This simile reminds me of Jim Rollins. Jim owned a
small farm back in West Virginia. His house was on a
piece of low land, right down at the mouth of a stream
that emptied into a larger river. Every few years storms
would descend, and at the fork where Jim's house stood
the rivers would overflow their banks and inundate his
property. Again and again his house was flooded, his
crops were destroyed, and the fences were washed away,
allowing whatever livestock had survived to wander off.

After the tragedy, Jim invariably began the work of
rebuilding. He would clean the mud out of the basement,
repair his fences, and proceed to plant other crops. In a
few years another flood was bound to descend, and the
process would have to be repeated all over again.

I often wondered why Jim didn't build his house on
higher ground. Actually, the house was located at the
very lowest point on the farm. Just back of the house
there was a high rise that would have been ideal for the
house. However, habit and sentiment bound Jim to the
location at the forks. His parents had built the house,
and while it had been flooded out a number of times, Jim
doggedly continued to rebuild it.

Picture with me another scene. The place is my office.
A young lady is sitting across from me complaining that
a third marriage is failing. Her name is Grace.

I asked Grace about her marriage, seeking especially
a description of the three men to whom she had been
wed. The temperaments of the three were very much
alike. They were all salesmen in one line or another.
Their educational backgrounds were quite similar. They
all loved a good time which, as she explained, "caused
me to be attracted to them."

One of the men had been married at the time this

young lady had met him. He had subsequently divorced his wife to marry her. It seemed that they all had roving eyes, for now husband number three wanted a divorce so he could in turn marry another woman.

"Why do I keep picking such lemons?" Grace asked. "I certainly don't want to marry a fourth time and have it go sour too!"

## The lowlands of mental conditioning

Grace's plight reminded me of Jim Rollins, and I told her about him. After explaining how the floods hit the lowlands periodically, I asked her, "Do you feel that this farmer should continue to rebuild in the same place or should he rebuild his home on higher land or even sell and move on?"

"I suppose," she replied, "that the sentimental attachment to the old homestead was strong, but Jim wasn't very smart to keep rebuilding on the same property."

"Exactly," I replied. "And, in a like manner, you have been building your life on the same emotional property year after year, bound by habit and sentiment to one similar marriage after another. However, you can prevent a further repetition of the pattern in a fourth marriage by moving to higher ground of thought and feeling. Some old habits may have to be broken and some new facets of temperament cultivated."

I explained how one's thoughts, attitudes, and feelings toward life become building blocks for tomorrow's experience. Trends of personality become submerged patterns that manifest themselves as events and conditions. Likes and dislikes become habits that dominate a person's choices in life. The English poet, George Crabbe, put it well in these lines:

Habit for him was all the test of truth;
It must be right, I've done it from my youth.[5]

Jim Rollins never questioned the wisdom of continuing to live where he and his parents before him had lived. Likewise, Grace never before questioned the quality of her marriage choices or why she had been attracted to

78

men whose tastes and temperaments were so similar. Just as the individual meets certain people because of where he travels on his daily rounds of office, club, and social group, so does he find friends, and make business associations because of the particular path he travels in mind. Whether the path be high or low, the individual meets and frequently marries people who are there on the path with him.

When someone like Grace finds herself continually rebuilding similar experiences in the lowlands of her personal kingdom where again and again tragedy repeats itself, she should look for entrenched attitudes and sentiments that unconsciously reassert themselves in the affairs of life. In various ways, she had become conditioned to traveling particular streets in mind that led her to the same dead end. She had met and married people whom she found along the same street of restlessness and discontent that she was on. Although Grace recognized that she had picked lemons, she had never considered that she was the lemon-picker.

## The conning tower of conscious perception

How had Grace's particular personality make-up, with its likes and dislikes, its engrained habits and responses, become submerged in her subconscious, drawing her again and again to unsuccessful marriages?

To understand this is to understand the nature of man's conscious and subconscious mind. Your conscious mind is like the conning tower of a submarine that has surfaced. The conning tower has five windows or apertures of objective perception—sight, touch, smell, hearing, and taste. Through these five windows of conscious awareness, you relate to the world around you. In relating, however, your responses are slanted by the way you feel subjectively. The subjective body-of-feeling that sways your objective responses springs from interior levels of memory, habit, drive, and instinct. These levels are the submerged portion of the submarine lying beneath the conning tower of consciousness.

You might think of man, at birth, as being a submarine that is completely submerged—conning tower and

79

all. His relationship to the world begins at the subjective level of feeling. He feels the comfort of his mother's closeness. He feels the satisfaction of a full tummy or the discomfort of an empty one. The submerged craft gradually surfaces from the subjective depths, and the infant becomes consciously aware of his world. The conning tower emerges, and the child begins to relate objectively with the environment around him through his five senses. The conscious mind becomes keener, and he begins to think, reason, analyze, imagine, and plan. The conscious mind, of course, is never separated from the subconscious lying below the surface. This brings up a point you must remember: Conscious thinking is always influenced by the subjective body-of-feeling that developed during early, impressionable years. Thus, your subconscious body-of-feeling somehow directs the way you consciously think and act now. Psychologists such as Alfred Adler believe that patterns laid down the first four or five years become inner impulsions which may determine the direction of conscious thought throughout the adult's life.

Early philosophers spoke of mind as a single, unitary thing with which man thought. By the late 19th century, psychologists began to make a distinction between conscious thinking and unconscious thought processes. It has become apparent now that mind operates as a dual function. The conscious is that phase of mind that objectively initiates new ideas, makes choices, entertains desires, and affirms images about the self. The subconscious is the subjective phase of mind that retains the ideas initiated, obeys the choices made, and acts to reproduce the images stored within it.

This dual process is what enables man to develop the unique skills and habits that make him individualistic. It enables him to move from desire to demonstration. For example, consider the person who wants to become a musician. His desire must be strong enough to become subjectified—to register with feeling on the submerged levels of memory, habit, and drive. Although the desire starts as a conscious process, it does not become demonstrated until the subconscious processes of mind take over. The desire drops first to the level of memory where

80

the desire is retained and remembered. As the individual practices on the particular instrument chosen, subjective habit reactions are formed that relieve him of detailed conscious effort. If persisted in, the desire finally becomes a drive that impels the individual toward his demonstration of a successful career in music. Hence, it may be said that as a result of a conscious desire, a person becomes not a conscious musician but a subconscious musician. The skill demonstrated is a subconscious response to a conscious desire.

### Your memory-laden subconscious mind

Because of the creative interaction of the dual processes of mind, it should be easy for anyone to move from desire to demonstration. It would seem that all he need do is initiate a desire consciously and persist in it until the subjective process of memory, habit, and drive take over, producing a demonstration. The theory is accurate and verifiable as may be seen by observing anyone who enthusiastically desires to become a typist, a pilot, a pianist, and the like.

However, in moving from desire to fulfillment in less objective areas, frequently something seems to go wrong. Much of the blame may be placed on the body of accumulated desire with which the subjective mind has become laden. Through the years, there has been a feeding of conflicting and inconsistent data into the subconscious. Conscious desires are often illogical. Perhaps, like Grace, a woman desires a stable marriage but illogically lets herself be attracted to an unstable, restless "good-time Charlie." Or perhaps a person longs for a change but illogically keeps plodding along Inertia Way or circling the Bog of Frustration. Such conflicting desires become submerged in the subconscious, and there they work at cross purposes. One desire cancels out another and no demonstration results.

If you could trace the path that desire takes as it moves from the conscious to the subconscious, becoming subjectified within, it would look much like the submarine-of-mind shown in Figure 4–2.

The thoughts of today are now on their way below deck

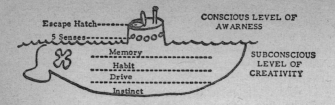

*Figure 4-2*

into the subjective area of retention. They pass first to the level of memory where desires and impressions are remembered. Repetition encourages them to become habit ways of thinking and reacting on the second level. If persisted in, such habits become drives and urges that serve as impulsions on the third level. Finally, drives that are deeply engrained and that stem from mass culture, society, and generic man exist at the instinct level.

Thus, as daily impressions and perceptions move below deck, they become submerged patterns that tend, in turn, to direct conscious thought. Of course, it is not every momentary thought or surface desire that becomes sub-jectified. Conscious thinking that is fraught with emotion or worry will be more virulent than casual thoughts. Conscious desires that are enthusiastic and imaginative will have more power than a fleeting fancy. Often an event of long ago will have more retentive vigor in the memory than happenings of yesterday. This is true of impressions of childhood that are prolonged into the present.

As the past recedes into the background, the weight of *memory residue* increases. As a result, the adult's sub-conscious may become memory-laden—weighed down by accumulated thought. Tragically, much with which the memory is laden may be illogical and inconsistent. Hence, the memory residue may serve to cancel out demonstrations instead of aiding in their realization. Still another tragedy may occur when the subconscious be-comes overweighed with false or negative memories that dominate the mind. Such thinking may not cancel out a demonstration, but it will manifest in demonstrated results that are negative.

The person who wishes to move from constructive

desire to demonstration must remember this: While the conscious is that phase of mind which initiates ideas and desires for the subconscious to act upon, the subconscious mind that becomes laden with inconsistent desires will produce naught. The subconscious that becomes overweighed with negative directives will usurp the rightful role of the conscious mind and negative responses will become automatic. The data stored in the subconscious does tend to react upon the conscious mind. If the conscious mind gives in to such influences and abdicates its right to rule, the subjective body-of-feeling takes on the role of directing.

When this reaction takes place, whether the individual is 20, 30, or 70 years of age, the conscious mind is no longer thinking but merely rethinking. Living becomes mechanical because new data have ceased to enter the mind. Today ceases to be a new day and becomes a memory-laden day premised on the impressions, feelings, prejudices, and attitudes of yesteryear. Life becomes monotonous, enervating, and repetitious. The spring of enthusiasm gives way to the winter of discontent.

### How to provide an escape hatch for habit thoughts

For Grace, life had become a monotonous repetition of one unsuccessful marriage after another. To prevent a further repeat performance, she had to break habit patterns that were dictating to her. She had to move to higher ground in terms of mature, consistent, stable thinking.

It is possible to replace old inconsistent desires with new ones, and thus provide an escape hatch for memories, impressions, and habit patterns that are not productive of happiness. The escape route is *recognition* and and it is through the conscious mind. A person must *recognize* and own up to desires that are illogical or negative before much can be done to change them. The person who nurtures hurt feelings, fondles his prejudices, or clings to his righteous indignations, will never be able to release them. However, once he sees them for the false, negative influences that they are, they will vanish through the honesty of his recognition. In their place, ideas that are constructive and logical must be entertained consciously. In turn, these will be subjectified and will activate the creative processes of the subconscious.

To provide an escape hatch for habit thoughts that may be voiding the demonstration of your desires, remember these points:

**1.** Submerged thought—as memory and habit—has selected the street on which you mentally live. If you find that street is not as attractive as you wish and the mental house in which the self resides leaves something to be desired, do not make the mistake of saying, "It's just my nature to be this way; I can't do anything about it." The mental house in which you live is simply an acquired nature. You acquired this particular nature under given conditions. Certainly, under other conditions, you can demonstrate a different acquired nature. Hence, you must provide those *other* conditions.

**2.** How do you recognize the habit thoughts that need to be released? Stand back from yourself and watch yourself walking. Does your walk proclaim that you are going someplace, or does it have the stoop of defeat that says you have been as far as you are going? Stand back and hear yourself talking. Listen to the content of your words. Are they critical and self-centered? Are they negative and self-defeating? Take a long look at yourself. Are you ill-tempered or impatient? Are you irresponsible or unstable? Let such undesirable facets of your acquired-self escape through the hatch of *recognition,* and then replace them with a new image.

**3.** Shakespeare offered wise advice when he wrote, "Assume a virtue though you have it not." [6] To build a new image, see yourself superior to the acquired nature that you have been calling *yourself.* To do this, you must separate the real self from the acquired. You must stop identifying with the acquired self, for to identify with it is to become submerged in it.

**4.** Learn to practice nonidentification. Disassociate yourself from undesirable habit-thinking. Mentally move away from the Streets of Resentment and Regret. Leave Inertia Way behind, and vacate the house on Self-Pity Place. You are under no obligation to stay where you are. Your present mental abode is like a rented house. If you were renting in an undesirable neighborhood and the agent for the house approached you and offered it for sale, you would be under no obligation to purchase it. You don't have to *buy* the place where you are. You don't have to identify permanently with it. Instead, non-identify with it by visualizing the place you want to be. Make a new identification, and let new desires move through you to new demonstrations.

5. Assume the virtue that you want to claim. Picture in your imagination the person you want to be. Visualize yourself possessing the qualities you deem desirable. Then, act *as if*. Act *as if* you were poised and self-confident. Walk *as if* you were a success. Talk *as if* you had empathy and regard for others. Soon you will genuinely personify the virtue you have assumed—the virtue you have subjectified.

Use Mental Data Processing Card No. 8 to help you identify habit-thinking that needs to be recognized and released. Then, assume the virtues you value by acting *as if*.

I now own up to habit thoughts that are negative, immature, or illogical. In all honesty, I identify and recognize undesirable images. My recognition provides an escape hatch for their release. In their place I now assume the virtues that I want to claim. I act as if they are already mine. As I personify these virtues, I move from desire to desired demonstration.

*Mental Data Processing Card No. 8*

## CHAPTER SUMMARY OF POINTS TO PONDER

1. As a physical being, you live in outer space—a limited time-place realm. As a mental being, the real you is unlimited for your living space is mind—a vast realm of infinite possibilities.

2. Within this limitless realm of inner space, you build barriers for yourself that obscure the splendor beyond the boundary. You settle down within that boundary and life becomes a routine thing.

85

3. The inner world of mind within that boundary may be likened to a city with its highways, byways, streets, and lanes forming the paths you travel in consciousness.

4. In your city of mind, you may be happy or miserable. The street on which you live may be Lonely Lane or Faith Way, depending on the habitual tone of your consciousness.

5. In your interior city of consciousness, you will discover that you frequent states of mind over and over, just as you do in outer living—traversing the same route to work, stopping at the same stores, and confining yourself to the familiar area of the city where you live.

6. Your mind—the inner house where you dwell in the city of consciousness—is furnished with a decor in keeping with the street on which you live. If your thoughts frequent Frustration Lane, you will find that you have not furnished your inner house with the brocades of confidence or the solid oak of self-esteem.

7. The mental images that bind you to the low-lands of achievement enter your inner realm of consciousness through the *conning tower of conscious perception.*

8. The images and data gathered into the conning tower of consciousness through the five senses become submerged in the subconsciousness as memory. It is the weight of this memory that acts as a barrier to your unlimited enjoyment of inner space.

9. The memory-laden subjective mind may become a force that directs conscious thought. When this happens, recurring patterns of thought and belief bind you to similar experiences over and over again.

10. These recurring habit thoughts may be eliminated from the subconscious mind through the *escape hatch of conscious awareness.* Habit patterns can no longer bind you and act as barriers when you expel them from your consciousness.

# CHAPTER FIVE

## How to Use the
## Cybernetic Action of
## Attraction

The young couple standing before me were obviously very much in love. They wanted to be married, and I suspected that they had come to ask me to perform the ceremony for them. It came as no surprise for I had been expecting Ron and Judy to take the plunge for some time.

I could not help remembering the unusual circumstances under which these two young people had met. I had known Judy for over a year and Ron for about that length of time. I remembered clearly the first time I saw them together. It was on the Coast, and they had arrived late for a lecture I was giving on Science of Mind. After the program, I learned of the violent circumstances of their meeting just that evening.

Judy was driving across town to my talk. Ron had driven up from the beach to attend the same lecture. As he entered the city, his car lost in a traffic bout with Judy's. When the dust settled, they learned that their destination was the same—which helped to smooth ruffled feelings—and Judy drove Ron to the lecture after his car was towed to a garage.

Breaking in upon my reverie, Ron was now saying, "Dr. Nichols, we want you to perform a wedding ceremony for us."

### How the magnetic lodestone of attraction works

I would not want anyone to drop this book immediately

and go in search of an accident, either with or without a car. I do not advocate this as an auspicious way of meeting your future mate.

I have no proof that these two people from different cities, on their way to the same destination, were involved in an accident so that they might meet and find a larger destiny together. However, I do know that there is a law operating in man's life, drawing to him his friends, his marriage partner, his business associates, and even the nuisances that sometimes plague him. This law acts like a mental lodestone, and, for Judy and Ron, the lodestone was love.

Webster's definition of lodestone also describes very aptly the magnetic properties of mind. A *lodestone* is a "magnetite possessing polarity; hence, that which strongly attracts." Possibly you have asked yourself why you attract the friends you do. In turn, have you wondered why you feel strongly attracted to one person and not to another? You find instant rapport with one person and, in his or her presence, you have a feeling of belonging—of having known him always. In the presence of another, the opposite may be true and you have no feeling of intimacy. No mental connection is made. Emerson once said, "My friends have come to me unsought. The great God gave them to me." [1] Like Emerson, there are qualities within you that attract to you your own.

THE MAGNETIC PROPERTIES OF MIND

Mind has magnetic properties that strongly resemble the polarity of a lodestone. Like attracts like. Dislike repels dislike. This is a universal principle. There is a cohesiveness between like molecules. A drop of water falling on a polished table rolls up in round, cohesive beads. Molecules of mercury exhibit this attractive quality dramatically. Just hold a drop of the liquid metal in your hand and see how it resists being separated into smaller droplets. Even as like molecules attract each other, like personalities attract each other because of the magnetic force of the similar properties in their structure.

This is not to say that the person to whom you are attracted will be similar to you in minute details, but in the sum total of his consciousness you will find values, aspirations, traits, and ambitions that are significantly like your own. These mental properties exert a magnetic pull upon you—a pull of attraction. The opposite can happen just as readily. Qualities of consciousness in another person that you find offensive will repel you. The mental chemistry of your consciousness functions as a cohesive force that holds to you that which belongs. That which does not belong will be repulsed by the polarity of your sum-total thinking.

For this reason, the type of friends and acquaintances you are attracting now will give you a clue to the state of your consciousness. Is the lodestone of your consciousness drawing to it constructive, optimistic, successful people who leave you feeling mentally stimulated after an evening together? Or is the lodestone of your sum-total thinking drawing to it negative, self-centered, critical, pessimistic people who leave you more depressed than you were before seeing them?

A curious thing often happens to people who begin to use the laws of mental cybernetics. They find that as their interest in new, mentally invigorating concepts expands, their circle of friends seems to change. Those who were only superficially entertaining drift away, and new, stimulating, like-thinking friends appear to take their place. As you grow toward mental maturity, associates who do not keep pace no longer interest you. At the same time, acquaintances who share your new knowledge and quest for self-discovery will stay within your circle of friends. Like attracts like.

## THE UNIVERSAL LAW OF ATTRACTION

To put this universal law of attraction in mental cybernetics terms, it may be said that: *Your sum-total consciousness is a cohesive factor that tends to attract like and repel dislike.* This means, in general, that the circumstances you experience in life are attracted and held to you by like properties in your sum-total thinking.

The lodestone of consciousness may be negative and charged with antagonism. Still, its properties attract. They attract the undesirable. The lodestone of consciousness may be positive and charged with enthusiasm, insight, confidence, faith, and love. It will attract that which belongs to it. That attracting force knows no boundaries or barricades. It reaches out beyond the confines of the immediate environment to fulfill the law of belonging. This it did for Ron and Judy. This it can do for you.

## The laws of invisible lines of belonging

You live in a mental universe where all things are drawn to their rightful place and held there by invisible lines of belonging. That you cannot see these lines is no proof that they do not exist. The tremendous lifting force of an electromagnet is invisible, yet the engineer who operates it knows it exists and can predict precisely what its pulling power is. The lines of belonging that hold the molecules of an atom together are as invisible as the atom itself, yet the physicist knows they exist and can change their structure to form new patterns of belonging.

Physical laws confirm that the action of attraction is present throughout the universe from the atom to the solar system. The earth and the other planets of our solar system are held to the sun by invisible lines of attraction that make the universe a predictable, dependable place of law and order. Earth is held to its rightful place without deviation, as evidenced by the constant length of its days and years. Its "rightful" place is that distance from the sun which is "right" for its weight and size. Astronomers see a definite pattern in the arrangement of the planets as they fan out from the sun. Closest to the sun is a relatively small planet—Mercury. Next come medium-sized planets—Venus, Earth, and Mars. Following these come the two largest bodies—Jupiter and Saturn. After these the order tapers off again to medium-sized Uranus and Neptune. And farthest out is the smallest planet of all—Pluto. Just as invisible lines of belonging tie the planets to the sun in a pattern that is "right" according to their structure, so lines of belonging draw to you that which is "rightfully" yours according to the structure of your consciousness.

Yes, the planets revolving around the sun are very

much like the personal circumstances that keep orbiting in your experience. Furthermore, there is another simile between man and the sun that has even more significance. The sun is a continuous creator, perpetually gathering new energy unto itself even as man may do.

Picture the solar system—the sun and its nine planets —orbiting as a unit through the larger galactic disk of which it is a part. According to physicist Fred Hoyle, author of *The Nature of the Universe,* as the sun moves through space, it sweeps up the thinly dispersed substance that is everywhere present and leaves a tunnel in its wake. As the sun moves through this spider web of substance, it gathers to itself all that is within the reach of its gravitational broom and uses it as fuel for constant creation. Hoyle estimates that the tunnel which the sun forms is a thousand times greater than the diameter of the star itself. Other scientists support this theory that each star is a creator which utilizes virgin substance from space to maintain a continuous process of renewal. Of this concept, Hoyle concludes: "I find myself forced to assume that the nature of the universe requires a continuous creation —the perpetual bringing into being of new background material." [2]

Even as a star is a gravitational center that attracts new substance to itself, the mind of man is a magnetic center—a center of consciousness—that moves through the greater field of universal mind. As the individual moves through this field of mind on his daily orbit of thinking, planning, hypothecating, visualizing, and imagining, he sweeps out a tunnel for himself and gathers in ideas from universal mind. However, he attracts only that which belongs to him—that which corresponds to the properties of his consciousness—and leaves that which is beyond the reach of his gravitational broom.

The length of that broom depends upon the intensity of man's consciousness. If it is charged with enthusiasm, insight, faith, and love, it will reach far out beyond the confines of the immediate environment to draw to it that which belongs. The consciousness that has been programmed with positive desires is highly charged, and, like Hoyle's star, may have a sphere of influence a thousand times greater than its own dimensions. Man, drawing upon the virgin stuff of universal mind, is a continuous creator. Through the law of attraction, his desires gather to themselves the ideas and substance necessary for their realization.

## The real meaning of consciousness

Describing consciousness in terms of similes helps to explain its nature. Yes, consciousness is your sum-total thinking that acts as a lodestone attracting like and repelling dislike. It is the gravitational broom of mind that sweeps to you all ideas within its reach. Now, let's take a look at the elements of which consciousness is composed.

Consciousness embraces both the real and the acquired. Latent within it are the high potentialities of the real self. However, superimposed upon that untapped inner self are all the acquired surface traits of the stand-in self. Thus, consciousness consists of both the real and the acquired.

Also, consciousness is both objective and subjective. Consciousness is not simply a product of the conscious mind, for, as you read in Chapter 4, the memories and habits programmed into the subconscious mind form a subjective body-of-feeling that sways objective responses. Thus, consciousness is a blend of objective awareness and subjective influences.

To summarize, consciousness may be defined as a center-of-awareness which is all that you are as an *offspring of life* plus all that you have become as an *experiencer of life*. It is this center-of-awareness that acts as your lodestone of attraction. This is your gravitational broom that sweeps to you the ideas and experiences that are "rightfully" yours—"right" for the structure of your consciousness as it is now constituted.

This suggests that your consciousness can be reconstituted to improve the things you are experiencing. The physicist can change the pattern of atoms in a molecule and alter its structure. You can change the pattern of thoughts in your mind and alter your consciousness. You can repel the undesirable and improve what "rightfully" belongs to you by "righting" your thoughts. You can attract the desirable by charging your consciousness with positive, dynamic, optimistic thinking that will draw greater power unto it. Those giant minds who have stood out in the mental galaxy of art, literature, and science—the great mental suns of history—must have swept out a wide tunnel in universal mind with the magnitude of their consciousness. However, there is no law saying that one person must be content with a gravitational broom which sweeps a tunnel only as large as a gopher hole while another sweeps with the attracting force of a sun. Nothing says this *except* the structure of man's consciousness—the nature of his center-of-awareness, his grasp of the real self, and his degree of mental unfoldment.

## Your radar thought beam

One of the great advances made in the electronic field in recent years has been the development of radar. The word *radar* is composed of the initial letters of the phrase *RA*dio *D*etection *A*nd *R*anging. Radar is a dramatic addition to man's sensory equipment, enabling him to detect objects such as aircraft and ships far beyond the normal range of sense perception.

Radar operates on an electric pulse system, with the transmitter and receiver working alternately. The transmitter is keyed to send out very short, very intense, bursts of energy. The time it takes for the echo to return, as the energy impulse strikes its object, can be used to determine how far away an object is, how fast it is going, and the direction it is taking. The system is put to a wide range of uses from the tracking of satellites to radar speed checks for traffic control.

The principle upon which radar operates illustrates a mental principle that functions in the law of attraction. Think of the brain as a radar transmitter and receiver and your thoughts as the electronic beams, and you have a true picture of your mind in action and how like attracts like.

Thoughts beamed from the pulse system of consciousness strike their objective and become reflected back to the sender. As like attracts like, fear thoughts will travel until they find an object to fear. Racing back, they will intensify the apprehension first broadcast. Success

93

thoughts will radiate until they find an object that will confirm success. Echoing back, they will intensify the positive consciousness originally sent out. Thoughts are empowered with an energy impulse that enables them to reach the right target and be reflected back to the transmitter.

The right target is that one which matches the nature of the thought. This explains why man so often meets his own thoughts in the minds of others. Under social distress, man is drawn to a soul brother who is experiencing like distress. In the heat of political controversy, man is attracted to those who share the economic theories that verify his own convictions. Invariably, the person who has a physical ailment will hear that it is "going around," and he soon finds others with whom to compare symptoms. Like attracts like.

You, as a radar-like beaming and receiving set, may entertain many thoughts that you have forgotten consciously. However, all of your thinking merges to form a composite beam that continues to transmit until changed. When that composite beam transmits on the frequency of love and enthusiasm for life, you are operating on the plane of consciousness with those who have loved and are loving now. This constructive body of consciousness will be the object that your thoughts strike and echo back from. If your composite beam is lowered to the depressing frequencies of worry, resentment, revenge, or hatred, you are transmitting on the plane of consciousness of those who are experiencing similar discord.

Some time ago the newspapers carried an account of a scientist who hoped some day to create a device that would pick up the voices of great men through the ages, perhaps reaching back to Socrates. Whether the spoken word of man still echoes in time is a matter for fanciful speculation, but what of the output of man's mind? Within the realm of possibility is the concept that each mind has its own particular wave length or frequency that could be picked up with a device sensitive enough to detect it. When you consider that, in the development of radar, the radio spectrum has been extended from 200 megacycles per second to over 20,000 megacycles per second, it seems reasonable to speculate that man's radar-like thinking apparatus may operate on a frequency that will some day be discovered. In any event, there is a mass consciousness that exists from the sum total of man's thinking, planning, behaving, and acting down through the ages. Love beamed forth from your mind operates not only on the frequency of those who embody a loving heart today but also on the frequency of those who through the ages worked for the love of mankind. The contrary, unfortunately, is just as true. Negative feelings beamed forth from you today echo back from a negative frequency built through the ages into the mass consciousness.

## How to develop directed thought beams

In defining consciousness earlier in this chapter, it was pointed out that your center-of-awareness consists of both the real and the acquired, of both objective and subjective thoughts. If you transmit only with this composite beam, then you are taking pot luck. To be sure what the results will be, it is wiser to develop a directed thought beam.

If subjectively you have been saying "fum-a-diddle" to things around you through the years, you are bound to have a lot of fum-a-diddle echoing back. No one can go through life disgusted without experiencing repeated conditions that call for disgust. No man can acquire an attitude of hatred toward a person, a nation, or a race, without having hatred reflected back to him.

Because you cannot be sure what acquired elements may go to make up your composite consciousness, develop a directed consciousness that is tailored to your desires. To do this, follow these pointers:

1. William James said, "The things we attend to come to us by their own laws." [3] By giving your attention to your desires, let your desired demonstration echo back to you. Tailor your consciousness to definite, specific purposes by turning the power of your attention to those purposes.

2. As attention illuminates the thing upon which it is turned, so, too, concentration gives a thing power and vitality. Concentration enables you to hold your attention on a certain desire long enough to let it germinate. Once germinated, a desire must be permitted to grow undisturbed by doubts or cross purposes.

3. Thus, a directed thought beam aimed at a specific desire and developed through attention and concentration must subsequently be released to find its target. It must be released to bounce off its objective and echo back as a demonstration in your experience.

Now, apply these three steps of *attention, concentration,* and *release* in the reconstituting of the nature of your consciousness with the affirmation on Mental Data Processing Card No. 9.

> With the tools of insight and optimism, I now alter the structure of my consciousness to form new patterns of belonging. I tailor my consciousness to purposeful ends by directing my attention and concentration wisely. I release this directed though beam and send it forth to find its objective and echo back to me as that experience which I desire.

*Mental Data Processing Card No. 9*

### The radar action of attraction

Observe your mind and you will see the radar action of attraction at work. You will see that every thought you send forth into the mental world has your return address stamped upon it. Your mind is a two-way radio, a walkie-talkie that sends and receives. The result, however, is more like a monologue than a two-way conversation for you hear, primarily, your own thoughts echoing back.

All thinking is productive of action. There are no lost thought beams. Your thoughts are reactive upon you. You cannot think ill of another without making yourself sick in some areas of your life—sick with worry, sick at heart, sick and tired, or even physically sick. Hatred directed toward another, even if it seems justified, becomes a hatred-bearer for the sender as it flashes back with radar precision. Its form may be altered, of course. Hatred may ricochet back as a feeling of despondency, irritability, nervousness, or even acid indigestion.

Because your thoughts react upon you, you should examine with care the things you transmit. Do you send forth hair-trigger thoughts of anger and resentment? Is the thought beam of your mind the carrier of pessimism or doubt? Do you transmit belittling, critical, and antagonistic attitudes to others? You cannot send forth a blessing or a depressing thought without having your own life blessed or depressed in some degree thereby.

### How to beam your thoughts for best results

Take a moment now to scan the radar screen of your consciousness. What are you thinking about? What were you thinking about an hour ago? Would you rate the state of your consciousness as primarily constructive or negative? If it is negative, your radar beam of thought is focused too low. You are too conscious of the things around you that appear imperfect. You are too conscious of lack, irritations, and problems.

There is a very important difference between "having a consciousness of" something and "being conscious of" something. For example, a person who is "conscious of money" is likely to have his thought beam focused so low that it bounces off the unpaid bills and mortgages piling up around him and echoes back as a feeling of financial desperation. On the other hand, the person who has a consciousness of money has raised his thought beam till it bounces off creative ideas for money-making and success. A person who is conscious of love is likely to notice its lack and lament his loneliness without it. The opposite is true for one who has a consciousness of love, for his thoughts are beamed lifeward and echo back to him as the joy of friends and companionship.

Thus, what you have a consciousness of tends to increase in your experience. As like attracts like, increase takes place. The law of attraction, therefore, also involves the law of growth. This means that the ideas you entertain tend to multiply, for thoughts and feelings have an affinity for other thoughts of a like nature. If you have a consciousness of good, your good will multiply. If you have a consciousness of self-improvement, the talents you develop will lead to the unfolding of other talents. If you have a consciousness of self-education, the courses you undertake will lead you on to ever-expanding areas of learning. Therefore, develop a consciousness of success, beam your thoughts lifeward, and let your success echo back and multiply.

### How to coordinate your thought beams for success

The difference between success and failure—personal, artistic, professional, literary, or financial—depends on whether or not you have achieved control of the thought beams of your mind. Success is the beaming of thought upward to constructive levels as mentioned above. Success is the *directed* beaming of thought, while failure is the *nondirected* diffusion of ideas.

Imagine, for example, that a plane is making an instrument landing during a storm. The pilot is depending upon a radar beam for guidance when suddenly there are several beams to follow. In such a case, a successful landing would be most difficult and might end in tragedy. The same thing happens in programming the mind for success. A person diffuses his energy by sending out thought beams in all directions and fails to arrive at a desirable destination in terms of peace of mind, health of body, and success in the affairs of life. However, the person who coordinates his thoughts, feelings, attitudes, drives and aspirations toward one directed goal is the person who is "on the beam." He will target in on his destination and land on direct center.

If your thought beams are to be coordinated, you must not only eliminate scattered thinking but hasty and impulsive action as well. It was pointed out when you started the study of mental cybernetics that inconsistent data cannot be programmed into an electronic computer. Similarly, hasty and incongruous ideas cannot be programmed successfully into the subconscious computer of mind. The person who conceives one idea and, before it is barely dispatched, impulsively changes his mind and sends off a countercommand will end up with nothing. In electronic programming, he would find of such data that "this does not compute." In radio transmitting, he would find that such data "jam" the airways, creating senseless and unintelligible static.

For example, in the case of radar, sufficient time must be given between one energy pulse and the next to permit one echo to be received before another pulse is sent forth. The interpulse interval of 1,000 microseconds enables radar to see targets 95 miles away. For a greater range, the interpulse interval must be correspondingly longer. So it is in the field of mind. There must exist between the transmission of one thought beam and the next sufficient time to permit the echo (answer) to be received. If man could see the jangled web of thought impulses emanating from his mind, he would understand why he fails to receive the good he desires from life.

When your desires reach to a goal that is somewhat distant, the thought beam that you direct toward that goal must be strong. In addition, your thought must be sustained long enough to bounce back to you with that which fulfills your desires. So, with all your mental, emotional, and imaginative power, center in on the goal you wish. Send your command and release it! Then wait patiently for your desire to return in manifested form before changing your mind or sending off a revised command. Perhaps the wisest words ever uttered were, "Be not anxious." The farther away the goal, the longer and stronger your desire must be.

### The atmosphere of your thought world

To some extent, every person has woven a tangled web of thought beams around himself. This web or atmosphere in his consciousness. Earlier in this chapter consciousness was defined as that which embraces both the real and the acquired—both the objective and subjective. It is the center-of-awareness in which man lives. If this sum-total thought atmosphere is constructive, it will impel man toward fulfillment. If it is negative, it restrains man from achieving his goals.

The thought atmosphere of mind is much like the atmospheric envelope surrounding the earth. It is necessary for life as we know it. It gives stability. It sustains life. In it, man carries on all the activities he has come to accept as natural. Although the gravitational and atmospheric envelope surrounding the world is one, yet each city has a distinct atmosphere that hovers over it. London occasionally has its black fog from the soft coal burned in the English hearths. Los Angeles has its smog. Pittsburgh has its smoke-tinted air. So it is with an individual. You have a consciousness hovering around you that is distinctive. It gives you stability. In it you carry on all of your mental activities. If your mental atmosphere is tainted with the smog of discouragement, if it is polluted with the impurities of guilt and self-doubts, or if it is gray with boredom, it is time to bring such feelings under control. It is time to raise your thought beams about yourself and break loose from a confining consciousness.

In the exploration of outer space, a major challenge that confronted technology was the problem of breaking free of the gravitational and atmospheric envelope surrounding the earth. However, science has now added this achievement to its growing list of impossible accomplishments. The atom has been split, the sound barrier has been broken, and now man has achieved a breakthrough of the atmosphere that tied him to the earth and has landed on the moon.

Can the same be accomplished for the mental atmosphere that confines the individual man to an established level of performance? The answer is yes. You can break free of patterns of thought that have restricted and limited you. You can break through to the pure, fresh air of mountaintop thinking. It will require a raising of your thought beams to higher, more constructive aspirations and keeping them focused there. Remember, your thoughts operate with radar-like action. They are beamed from the pulse system of your mind to strike their objective and reflect back to you. This network or web of outgoing and incoming thoughts constitutes your atmosphere-of-consciousness, and, to raise its level, you must keep your outgoing thinking high.

Through his mental atmosphere, each one attracts to himself that which belongs and repels from himself that which does not belong to his consciousness at that moment. To alter or break free of this mental enclosure is to find a new life.

### How thought barriers are built

Man's mental atmosphere begins to develop at birth or possibly before. There are those in the psychiatric field who believe that prenatal influences may be significant. Be that as it may, at birth a child begins to sense the mental quality of the home into which he is born. If love, respect, understanding, and gentleness abound, these qualities will influence the budding consciousness of the child. If constructive attitudes are absent and the mental tone is one of distrust, hostility, or indifference, this atmosphere infects the young mind, for thoughts are contagious. This atmosphere is the beginning of the child's mental envelope or thought barrier, and it tends to bind him to the very attitudes displayed by his parents.

Through the years, this individual will attract what belongs to his mental atmosphere or aura—things which may be quite different from what he objectively wants. He may go through life cursing his bad luck, critical of others who misunderstand his intentions, and angry with the gods who do not seem to smile favorably upon him.

Until he discovers laws such as these set forth in mental cybernetics, such a person does not know that the cause of his frustration is within him and that he carries it wherever he goes in the form of a personal mental atmosphere. Since it is the nature of the ego to justify itself as a means of self-protection, the individual looks outside himself for the cause of his failure. He rationalizes and finds logical reasons for his business fiascoes. He places the blame for inadequacy upon parents or lack of opportunity. If he can find a plausible scapegoat, he will go through life kicking the goat and remaining unhappy, unloved, and unpopular. However, as the astronaut was confined to earth only until a breakthrough was made in the gravitational and atmospheric barrier, man is restricted to a limited consciousness only until he learns that his thought atmosphere is holding him back.

### How a failure consciousness is built

How is a failure consciousness built? It may extend back to childhood when a feeling of rejection was embodied in the child's mind. Perhaps he was deprived of a feeling of approval from adults and grew up in the absence of love. As an adult himself, he may now hold himself aloof from the crowd so that he will not be hurt again. He fears disapproval and may feel that he does not belong. Others sense this and find him difficult to like. His negative consciousness advertises itself to one and all. Silent though it is, it communicates itself as an invitation for rejection. In his home, at work and in organizations, he will find a response that validates his feeling of rejection. Others will unconsciously reject him because of the unwritten but unmistakable sign that hangs over the door of his consciousness.

### CASE HISTORIES OF A NEGATIVE AND POSITIVE CONSCIOUSNESS

Consider the person who feels he or she is not liked— the person who has an I-have-no-friends attitude. How does that attitude function to attract loneliness and repel friends? Let's take the case of Ann who has enveloped herself in a consciousness of self-depreciation and feels that others are too busy to bother with her.

Ann is walking down the street. She sees Claudette coming toward her. Ann unconsciously says to herself, "There comes Claudette, but she probably will walk right by me without noticing me." As Claudette comes closer, something in a store window catches her eye and she walks by Ann without seeing her. In such a situation, there is no rapport, no mental contact, even though they may have been only a few feet apart.

Let us look at another girl whom we shall call Edna. Edna has a radiant, friendly consciousness that takes in both sides of the street. She sees Claudette window-shopping as she strolls toward her. Claudette's attention seems riveted on a display of French Room hats. But, as Edna gets closer, Claudette's gaze is pulled away from the hats and is drawn toward Edna. Something about Edna's presence has reached out and tapped Claudette on the shoulder. Her friendly atmosphere has silently called: "Yoo-hoo, hello there! Look this way. Here I am!"

Both Ann and Edna have invitations hanging over the doors of consciousness. Ann is saying, though unconsciously, "I don't have friends. No one loves me. People ignore me." This is an invitation for rejection.

Edna is saying, "I like people. I have many friends. People like me and I'm accepted everywhere." This is an invitation for acceptance.

Edna is expressing the real self—that wonderful, special, radiant, successful self that is potential within each person. Ann is expressing an acquired self that is falsely built on imperfect knowledge about herself.

Success is a universal fact. Atoms succeed as they orbit perfectly in the heart of every molecule. Creation succeeds as life comes forth in its wondrous array of forms. The galaxies succeed as they circle flawlessly through the heavens. Success should be, and must be, a personal experience for you too. Every person is filled with a success potential. Each person, however, must take the steps necessary to turn this potentiality of success into a reality. He must melt down this universal success-potential into the individual coin of ability, creativity, and constructive activity. When failure occurs, it occurs at that point where man pours universal power into the molds he has created with his individual mind.

## How to create a success aura

A dictionary defines *aura* as "1. Any subtle, invisible emanation or exhalation; 2. A distinctive atmosphere surrounding a person; 3. *Elec.* A draft, or motion of the air, caused by electric repulsion, as when the air near a charged metallic point is set in motion." [4]

Down through the ages, man has sensed individuals who possessed a distinctive thought atmosphere or consciousness. Artists often depicted this as an aura or visible halo around the heads of saints. It is significant that they painted the aura as a round disk, for the circle has been used as a symbol from ancient times. According to psychologist, Carl G. Jung, the circle is a commonly recurring symbol in dreams. Symbolically, the circle denotes integration of the personality—maturity, stability, insight, self-fulfillment, and completion. Thus, it may be inferred that the aura pictured around the heads of great personages denotes their integration with the over-all purpose of life.

Does the aura belong exclusively to the lofty and the sainted? Not in the broader sense, for as explained in this chapter, each person lives within a thought atmosphere that accompanies him wherever he goes. It is true, however, that one aura may glow with radiant splendor while another is feeble and bedimmed. It is true that some individuals possess a "success aura." They have that almost magical attractive force called charisma.

The magnitude of the "auric" force enveloping you will depend on your degree of integration with the real self. To the extent that you can discard imperfect, inadequate, false images about yourself and program into your consciousness the radiant potentialities of the real self, you will move toward a powerful, integrated, fulfilled personality. The aura you build will be like a magnet that selects iron filings from sand. It will select for you that which belongs and leave behind, like untouched grains of sand, that which does not belong to you.

STEPS IN BUILDING A SUCCESS AURA

To build your success aura, follow these steps:

1. Don't buy the idea that some people "have it" while others do not. It is true that some people seem to enjoy an outstanding portion of popularity, personal magnetism, charisma, and the like. But, where one man's success may

depend on social extroversion, another's may depend on quiet introspection as an author, composer or philosopher. You "have it." You have the principle of success within you and can demonstrate it in some productive form!

**2.** Know that you can expand the aura that surrounds you. Reach out with imagination, enthusiasm, and confidence and draw a larger circle. Improve its quality and its color by removing the negative impurities of discouragement and self-pity from your consciousness. Don't be content with the size of your present consciousness, for the same circle will bind the same life to you.

**3.** Beware of the things you don't like. No one has become successful by dwelling on failure. No one becomes happy by singing a sad song. If you don't like to hear of others' operations, don't give an "organ" recital yourself. If you don't like poverty, don't accept the fallacy that there is something virtuous about being poor. The universe has never initiated a poverty program or taken bankruptcy. Daily you should meditate on the lavishness of nature and imbibe this spirit until you make it your own.

**4.** Look to the goal you want to achieve. Keep your mind nourished by thoughts about that goal that are uplifting and optimistic. It is not enough to say, "I want to be successful." What do you want to succeed at—what career, what profession, what personal talents, what interpersonal relationships? If you want to be healthy, visualize what you are going to do with that health. If you want confidence and personal charm, visualize yourself using that confidence and charm creatively.

I now close my eyes and picture a warm, golden radiance emanating from my being. It is my consciousness of wholeness, happiness, and success. Though invisible, this aura blesses me as I move forth in its embrace and draws to me the perfection, power, confidence, charm, and success that belong to the real me.

*Mental Data Processing Card No. 10*

**5.** Do not leave the "action" out of the radar action of attraction. If you are to attract the things you want, you must do the muscular. You must take the realistic steps and perform the acts necessary to the demonstration. One of those acts is the disciplining of your mind through the daily affirmation of Mental Data Processing Card No. 10.

## CHAPTER SUMMARY OF POINTS TO PONDER

1. The mind of man is like a lodestone that possesses magnetic properties which correspond to its polarity. Hence, like thoughts attract like people and conditions.

2. The people and conditions around you "belong" to you at this moment for they are held to you by the attracting force of your present thoughts and feelings.

3. Those thoughts and feelings act as a gravitational force that gathers to you all that belongs to the sum total of your consciousness, be it constructive or negative.

4. The sum total of your consciousness is like a radar transmitter constantly scanning life around you for the "right" target. The target it strikes and re-echoes from is the one that matches the nature of your consciousness.

5. If the properties of your consciousness are attracting the undesirable, you can alter your thoughts and reconstitute the structure of your consciousness along positive lines.

6. Success or failure depends primarily on whether you have achieved control of your thought beams.

7. Controlled, directed thought helps keep you "on the beam" as you pursue your goal. Nondirected thought diffuses your energy and results in failure.

8. When the goal you desire is somewhat distant, the thought beam that you direct toward it must be strong and well-sustained.

9. Remember that to some extent everyone has

built a tangled web of thought beams that cancel each other or diffuse one's energy.

10. To escape from this web, watch both your incoming and outgoing thought beams and discipline your mind to mountain-top thinking.

# CHAPTER SIX

*Your Magic Power
of Imagination with
Mental Cybernetics*

Following a spell of rainy weather in the Pacific North-west, the press carried this account of a near tragedy. A man and his dog had gone for a walk along a beautiful, isolated stretch of Oregon coastline. At one spot along the cliff, the man stopped with his faithful canine friend to gaze out over the ocean.

He was admiring the surf as it beat against the shore far below him when, quite suddenly, the point of land on which he stood gave way and plunged downward toward the water. Fortunately, the section under foot did not break up completely, and he and his dog stayed atop as it sank. When it stopped, he turned to see a perpendicular bank of 12 to 15 feet isolating him from the top of the cliff and the road which was some distance away. Below him another straight drop made descent impossible.

The man surveyed the situation in which he found himself. The wall seemed impossible to scale, and he wondered how long he would have to wait to be rescued. It was not a populated area or even a portion of the coastline along which many people walked. His thoughts raced ahead, and he could see himself isolated for days before being found. As he lived alone, it might be a week before anyone missed him. Fear began to take possession of him.

He called out for help, yelling as loud as he could in the hope that someone would be within hearing distance. Frantically, he tried again and again to scale the muddy, water-soaked bank that stretched above him. But the rains that had loosened the soil and caused the slippage made the wall too slick to climb. Over and over the thought pounded in his brain, "What if no one should find me!" Night came and with it exhaustion from his futile attempts to scale the wall that separated him from safety. His voice had become hoarse from screaming in competition with the pounding surf. His calls were now so weak that no one would have been able to hear him.

What was his canine friend doing all this time? The dog, too, had looked around and surveyed the scene from the ledge. Finding no way to leave the small, isolated point, it lay down to rest. Occasionally it looked up and watched its master's futile attempts to climb the bank or cocked its head at his shouts. The dog accepted the situation without question. In its mind, no image of starvation welled up to panic it. Its thoughts did not race ahead with the speculation that it might be stranded for days with no chance of escape. Lacking the imaginative powers of its master, the dog relaxed and waited without anxiety or tension.

The press reported that the next morning a boy, out for a romp with his dog along the cliff, came close to the landslide. He was busy throwing sticks for his dog to retrieve when the two dogs saw each other. Looking down, the boy saw the man and dog on the ledge below and brought rescuers. The man was rushed to the hospital in a state of serious shock and exhaustion. The dog was fresh and unharmed—none the worse for his stay on the isolated point of land.

## Imagination—the characteristic mark of man

One factor that distinguishes man from the lower orders of life is the imaginative faculty. Used rightly, this power is creative. It has created the civilization mankind enjoys today. It has created beauty in the form of paintings, poetry, literature, and sculpture. It is the inspiration of the artist and the saint. It has given wings to the mind of man.

But imagination can also be misused. It can be used negatively. Through fear, it can create a torture chamber for the mind. It can create a "Dante's Inferno" or a heaven of infinite beauty.

Man can use his imagination to build mighty sky-scrapers, bridges to span rivers, complex machinery to turn the wheels of industry, and rockets to carry him to the moon. But he can also use his imagination to create panic and desperation, to produce failure, to create un-happiness, and to belittle his powers of mind.

Imagination is not absent from the lower orders of life, but there it expresses itself as instinct. It is more a col-lective faculty than an individual, volitional faculty. For example, the nests that birds build differ widely, from the spherical mud home of the swallow to the fiber cup of the hummingbird, delicately woven from plant down and spiderweb. Birds of one species, however, built their nests very much like other birds of their species. Through collective imagination, they have evolved the nest style best suited to their kind, and this they build year after year. Their imagination conforms to a "set" pattern. Their nesting habits have been programmed to this set through previous collective experience.

There is not much deviation from this set in the lower orders. The beaver builds a unique house with an under-water entrance for security. To construct his house, he first needs to dam up a stream. Instinct, evolved through creative imagination, enables the beaver to build his remarkable ponds. When conditions change, however, imagination does not respond with the same immediacy in the lower order as it does in man. Imagination patterns hold the beaver to the set way he has been building his dams for centuries.

The naturalist, Alan Devoe, once observed a young family of beavers attempting to build a dam. They had chose a swift-flowing stream that again and again defied their efforts at pond construction. Soon an older beaver appeared on the scene to help them, and Devoe concluded that they had sent away for the old dam-builder. Appar-ently the young beavers did have enough imagination to call for an expert. In spite of this, the dam-construction of the beaver and the nest-building of the bird remain much the same for, below man, imagination operates mainly on a species or collective achievement level.

110

Man, however, is not a bird. He is not a beaver. Man is not required to build his nest as his parents built theirs. He is not required to erect a dam and construct a house patterned exactly after the home of his fellow creatures. By means of imagination—imagination functioning at the greater freedom that belongs to man—he can construct a different kind of life than any he has known in all the centuries that have gone before. Man is free to roam the universe. He is bound to no "set" ways of doing, unless he falls victim to previous limiting patterns that restrict his freedom of imagination.

## The magic of imagination

Man's progress is moving today at an accelerated pace. The latest designs in engineering and in current technological know-how will be obsolete in a very few years. One scientist has said that about half of what a graduate engineer has learned will be obsolete in a decade. Furthermore, he declared that "half of what that same engineer will need to know ten years from now is not available to him today." [1]

The boundlessness of man's imaginative faculty is illustrated by the fact that knowledge and technological achievement doubled in the 150-year period between 1750 and 1900. This increase represents a doubling of all scientific progress made by man in all the centuries prior to that time.

From 1900 to 1965, technological achievement doubled again—not just a doubling of the previous 150 years' achievements but of *all* accomplishments of the ages. In the 35 years from 1965 to 2000, scientists envision another knowledge explosion that will again double scientific progress.

What is responsible for this breath-taking acceleration of scientific achievement? It is nothing other than the *magic of imagination*. The magic of new ideas and new breakthroughs in thinking have created a different world from that known by parents and grandparents.

Can man bring the same advances into other areas of life? Can man by means of imagination, rightly applied, bring peace to the world? Can he lift his life out of pov-

111

erty—out of the limitation he has known—and plant his feet upon a new highway to confidence and power? The answer of mental cybernetics is an emphatic *yes!* Yes, if man can learn to control his imagination. Yes, if he becomes the creative director of it and not the victim of it—as was the man on the cliff.

## The creative power of mind

To understand man's mental processes, let us categorize them into four areas or functions. These are the distinguishing features of man's mind:

1. The reflective faculty—the ability to observe specific data and synthesize new conclusions from the data observed (inductive reasoning).
2. The faculty of reason—the ability to analyze a general conclusion and arrive at specific consequences, thereupon deciding between those consequences (deductive reasoning).
3. The retentive faculty—the ability to memorize and recall experiential data.
4. The imaging faculty—the ability to visualize, to foresee, and to generate new ideas, based more upon an intuitive process than a process of inductive or deductive reasoning.

Of these four, the development of the last is most vital to any degree of success in life. Imagination—the artistic functioning of the mind—is the creative activity of life. The powers of reflection, retention, and reason put acquired data of past experience to use, but it is by means of imagination that original ideas are formed into new patterns and become the outpictured *new* conditions in life.

A dictionary defines *imagination* as: "The act or power of imagining; formation of mental images of objects not present to the senses, especially of those never perceived in their entirety; hence, mental synthesis of new ideas from elements experienced separately." [2] Imagination is this, but perhaps it is more than this! It is reasonable to believe that this faculty of the mind springs from a

112

universal source or a universal imagination that has projected the cosmos, in its myriad forms, into being.

Looking around, it becomes apparent that an intelligent, cohesive energy is everywhere present, from the nucleus of the atom to the heart of man. Let us call this creative, intelligent, cohesive energy that pervades the universe "mind." This universal "mind," creating the endless variety that it does, must embody the ultimate essence of imagination. That essence is passed on to each form which universal mind pervades. It comes forth in the animal as the instinctual imaginative patterns that it has evolved. It comes forth in man as the individual, volitional power to visualize, originate, and project new images into creation.

To put it another way, it might be said that "man is made in the image and likeness" of the universal mind that pervades everything. As universal mind can produce endless variety, so can man, using the likeness of that mind within him, produce endless original ideas. Hence, his imaginative powers need not be restricted to Webster's definition that entails a new synthesis from old experience. The higher reaches of man's imagination supersede experience and tap, intuitively, the ultimate essence of universal imagination. Thus, the imaginative powers of man are as limitless as the cosmos itself. Man is a miniature reproduction of the cosmic process of creation. He is a microcosm with in macrocosm of mind. In his own world, he is an original creator, a director, a producer of his personal drama of life. What is that drama like?

## Your movie corporation of consciousness

Life, as you have imagined it to be through the years, is now programmed into your consciousness as a permanent, personal, daily drama. It is much like the roadshow engagement of a popular film that stays at the local cinema for an extended run of two or three years. Your days are composed of reels of film which you have taken with the camera of imagination, and memory runs them over and over again.

You, as producer of your drama-of-life, are like a

movie corporation. You are an M-G-M, Inc. or a Columbia Pictures Corporation. You are free to specialize in any kind of picture you choose—lighthearted musical comedies, heavy psychological dramas, Westerns, or horror movies. What trend has your production taken? Through the years have you pictured yourself as one denied the opportunities of life that are lavishly bestowed on others? Have you starred yourself as the fall guy, the villain type, the Ned Sparks dead-pan character, or the hero-who-gets-the-girl type?

Imagination can be your greatest creative tool or your number one hindrance. It will be your handiest tool if you use it to impress the mind with that which you really want to become. Like a movie producer who wishes to film a constructive, lighthearted story, you must focus your imaginative powers upon images of yourself that are complimentary, encouraging, and constructive. However, if you are a producer who has specialized in tragedies, you will have an eye that is trained to look for the seamy side. All too often, reel after reel has been ground out in man's youth and young adulthood picturing him as inadequate, void of ability, and failure-prone. Such mental films, if rerun frequently in consciousness, can act as a forced hindrance to success.

## Refilming the old rerun

How do you turn imagination into a constructive tool? How do you turn off the old reruns that crowd your viewing schedule and demand prime time?

There are some primary concepts about yourself that you must understand in using imagination to program your mind for success: First, you cannot change the old, negative films produced by you in the past by turning them off objectively. You cannot change the rerun being broadcast from the studio simply by snapping off your television set. You must go to the inner studio of mind and refilm the reels that are undesirable. In other words, you must go to the inner source—to the cause—from which the effects flow. Remember, one of the basic laws of mental cybernetics is: *A principle of cause and effect governs all creation. To create anew, you must initiate new causes from which new effects will flow.*

If your objective life today seems to be a parade of inadequate experiences and financial struggles, you may feel that this inadequacy is very real. You may feel that the "real form" is the outer thing—the level of supply, the state of your affairs, the figures in your bank book. These things, however, are real only as effects. The "real forms" of external, outer experiences are actually within you as images. The cause, the source, the beginning of the outer, is within you. And, it is within you that creative imagination can mold new images and new causes which will be projected as new outer effects.

You will continue to view the same objective conditions —the same old reruns—until you make a new mental movie. Imagine a seamstress who continued to cut her material from an out-moded dress pattern year after year! She will continue to wear the same unstylish garment until the originating pattern is changed. The inner pattern is the real form, and to change the outer, objective result, you must introduce a new inner pattern. You must recast the image within into a more complimentary role for yourself. You must film a new movie in your inner studio of awareness. On this fresh reel you must depict a new self-conception and self-definition. You must discover and uncover within you a new self-image. You must redefine and redesign your interior conception of yourself. You must replace any role in which you have cast yourself as inadequate with a vision of the real self. You must break former contracts with your acquired, stand-in self and hire the real star. You must give your real self prime billing in your drama-of-life. Above all, you must have faith and confidence in the real self and in its ability to carry you to stardom.

### Separating the picture from the producer

Next, in using imagination to program your mind for success, you must not confuse the picture taken with the picture taker. As the picture taker, as the producer, you are greater than your production. You always transcend what you have projected. You are superior to it and

115

have command over it. Therefore, you have the power to change the results that your thinking has produced. Separate the producer from the picture, and begin your rewrite of the character you wish to portray.

Too many people are playing false roles—acquired parts that do not reveal the real self. Perhaps you've heard it said of a self-conscious person, "She's really very nice when she forgets herself." Or, of a quiet, restrained individual the remark may be, "He is wonderful when you get to know him." How true this is! Often you must dig beneath the acquired, unreal self before you find the real person. People imagine themselves to be something they are not and present this image to the world. Sometimes they do it to protect the ego. They do it to compensate for assumed inadequacies, hostilities, and various complexes. In every case, they are casting the real self in a false role and saying, "This is what I am."

To break free of this false practice, you must stop identifying yourself with false, uncomplimentary roles. You must not say, "This is what the producer is like." The producer is not the film produced. Alfred Hitchcock is not "Psycho." Separate yourself—as the producer—from the production, and begin a retake of the images you have programmed into mind.

## HOW TO TRAIN YOURSELF IN THE USE OF BASIC CONCEPTS

You may ask, when using the tool of imagination, "Am I to understand that when you speak of changing one's self-image, you mean the substitution of a better self-image for that of an inferior one? And, if so, am I not trading one picture for another?" Separating the producer from the picture is not trading one self-image for another. It is, however, training yourself in the use of these basic concepts about the real you:

**1.** You must recognize that what you have accepted through the years as being *you* has simply been a picture gallery formed around you. A realization of this fact is the beginning of real change.

**2.** In divorcing the producer from the production, you break the binding identification of yourself as a certain type with a set personality and set abilities. You assume your rightful command as producer, and your life becomes fluid. The experiences that bound you to an inadequate level fall away like chains from a prisoner, and you find yourself free to create anew.

**3.** In this freedom, as if becoming a child again, you have a fresh opportunity to form new self-images. But, more important, those self-images hopefully will capture the real self. For the first time you will stand in the presence of the "real." Rather than trading one self-image for another, mental cybernetics consists of getting rid of the unreal, the untrue, or to coin a word, un-you.

Use Mental Data Processing Card No. 11 to separate you, the producer, from the production you have been viewing.

As producer-director, I now assume command of my life. I discard the old script and cast off inadequate portrayals. With fresh inspiration and imagination, I expose a new self-image on the film of consciousness. This new self-concept captures all the power, perfection, poise, and mastery of my real self. This new self-image carries me to stardom in all my affairs.

*Mental Data Processing Card No. 11*

## Your magic power of imagination

"But," protested the young lady sitting across the desk from me, "wouldn't I just be lying to myself?"

Carol and I had been talking about the use of imagination in changing one's self-image. She found the concept hard to buy and objected. "You are suggesting that I say something about myself which is not true. How can I tell myself that I am attractive when I know I am not? How can I affirm that I am a friendly, outgoing person when I find it so difficult to meet people. You are asking me to pretend that I am attractive and have a friendly, easy-to-meet personality. I am not like

117

that. It wouldn't be true. How can I believe it when it isn't true?"

"Well, Carol," I countered, "you tell me what the truth about you really is."

"I'm plain," Carol replied. "I find it difficult to make friends. I'm something of a square. When I am with a boy, conversation is painful. I don't know what to say. I just don't sparkle. After a few dates, or—let's face it— after the first date, I'm dropped."

She paused with a dejected sigh, and I probed, "Is that really the truth about you?" Continuing, I asked her to explain how this self had become a reality for her. She responded that she had always been this way. She felt she had been born with this nature. This was the only kind of person she had ever known as herself, so it must be her true self.

I pointed out that this person she called her "true self" had been constructed in exactly the same way I wanted her to construct a superior self. "This that you call true, Carol, has been built up through the years as you constantly affirmed that you were plain, withdrawn, and unsociable. If you affirm that you are attractive, friendly, poised, and outgoing, you will not be lying to yourself—you will be negating the lies you have been telling yourself for too long. "It may also be," I reflected, "that others had a part in telling you these lies. If as a child you were encouraged to be seen and not heard, perhaps you never learned to be sociable. Possibly you never had a chance to sparkle!"

### How to listen to a talking picture of you

I explained to Carol that man lives in a mental universe which honors his thinking about it, be it positive or negative. He sees the projection of his thoughts as things and experiences. This is not to say that the things he sees are not real. They are, relatively. Thoughts are real, and the things projected are as real as the thoughts that project them. But, just because a thing is real, it is not necessarily true. It may be true, or it may be false, according to its nature.

"Carol," I remarked, "you are too young to remember

a song entitled "If I Had A Talking Picture of You" but do you realize that no matter how silent you are, your feelings and actions are talking about you to others? Each person is actually a talking picture. Wherever you go and whatever you do, you are telling others about yourself."

After a little self-reflection, Carol had to admit that she was a literal walking-talking picture of the image she had of herself. I suggested that she answer these questions frankly: What sort of person do I believe myself to be? What image do I convey to others? What image do I perpetuate of myself as a person, as a friend, as a dinner companion, as a theater partner, and as an office co-worker? Do I project a self that others find disagreeable? Or do I impart an image of friendliness, empathy, and sincerity?

"Remember," I finished, "whatever that image is, it is indeed a 'talking picture of you.' You cannot hide it. You can only change it." This was the solution for Carol. It is the solution for you. You must get rid of the un-you.

### How to develop concepts of a superior image

The *image* you must work with and change is not a thin veneer. It is the deep-down concept you have of yourself. In every contact you make in life, this "talking picture" is saying something about you. If it is constructive, it is saying pleasant things about you. If it is negative, it is saying unlovely things about you. Your image speaks for itself. You cannot hide it, but can change it.

To change your self-concept into a superior image, you must start paying court to the qualities you admire. Make it a deliberate courtship. Entertain the qualities you wish to develop. The girl who wishes to gain poise and charm would do well to take a course at a reputable modeling school. The man who lacks force and self-confidence when leading a club meeting would do well to sign up for public speaking. To court a new concept of yourself, you must develop a sense of belonging. You must come to feel that the qualities of your choice belong to you.

Make the courtship as realistic as that of a boy courting the girl of his choice. The young man will call the
girl, take her to the movies, ask her to go dancing, and
entertain her in various ways which show her that he
cares. A growing feeling of closeness develops, with
marriage the possible result. In like manner, you must
entertain the qualities you desire when starting the
courtship of the concepts of self-adequacy, confidence,
poise, and personal dynamism. You must build an intensity of desire and a feeling that the object of your
choice belongs to you. If you succeed, a marriage takes
place on the mental plane with the concepts you have
courted.

Too many are courting the concept of being unloved
or unlovely, of being inadequate and inept. Ask yourself
the question, "Have I been carrying on an undesirable
courtship with discouragement, irritation, fear, worry,
and limiting ideas? Have I been paying court to belittling
thoughts of myself and criticism of life?" If so, end the
courtship immediately before it culminates in marriage
to unhappiness, loneliness, and limitation.

### The value of self-visualization

How do you pay court to a new quality? You see
yourself possessing it. Of course, as mentioned in the
preceding paragraph, do *all* you can on the experience
level to guide the development of the new quality. Take
instruction in public speaking if you do not know how
to project your voice beyond the first row. But of equal
importance is the mental work you should do to *see*
yourself in a new role. This mental work puts your
imagination to use in visualization.

Take fifteen minutes daily to visualize yourself going
through the actual motions you would perform if you
possessed the quality you desire. For example, Carol, the
young lady who wished to be more skilled in conversation,
took time each day to see herself in situations where she
conversed brilliantly and radiated a grace that charmed
those around her. She practiced silent but vivid conversation, using the power of imagination to change her
concept of herself. It worked! People began to find her

120

attractive—not because she had altered her features but because she had altered her self-image. A superior image of herself now became the walking-talking picture that people saw.

## A CASE HISTORY OF THE POWER OF VISUALIZATION

Recently I visited a friend who was confined to the hospital for a short time. Carl had come to this country from Germany as a young man, and, as we talked, he started reminiscing about his boyhood in Germany many years ago and how he had dreamed of coming to the golden West to be a cowboy. He had been highly imaginative as a boy and had painted vivid mental pictures of himself visiting this new land that he longed to see. His desire to emigrate finally impelled him to stow away on a ship that was embarking for Canada. Upon landing, he was detained by the immigration authorities for a time. While waiting, he spent hours lassoing a pole in the yard where he was confined. Mentally, with the power of imagination, he was courting the concept of himself as a cowboy. On the experience level, he was also preparing by developing the rope skills he would need.

Shortly after the Canadian authorities released him, he came to the United States and experienced the thrill of seeing the places he had dreamed of for so long. He went west soon after the turn of the century and found work on a ranch in Wyoming. He became the cowboy that he had dreamed about in his native land. For 14 years he lived in the fulfillment of that dream, before his creative imagination carried him into a new career as an artist and decorator.

Carl said to me at the hospital, "You know, I sincerely believe that if I could draw a picture of health as clearly and as definitely as I drew a picture of myself becoming a cowboy, I would be well." Carl was right about the power of visualization. His demonstration as a young man was forceful testimony to the use of imagination in building a self-image of one's choice. Then, too, he had prepared himself with skills on the experience level that reinforced his mental visualizing. He had done both the mental and the muscular. These same composite factors apply in the area of health.

Through the power of visualization, you draw pictures of yourself. You paint conceptions of the meaning and purpose of life. These patterns of visualization show up in the state of your health, in the way you express your abilities, and in the attitudes you hold toward life. The way your life shall go is generally determined in the visualizing room of your mind—in that mental room where imagination paints and sketches your desires. Those desires that are deep and emotionally charged become the urges that motivate you. They set in motion the trends of your experience.

## Visualization is an emotional process

One of the first things to be realized is that visualization is an emotional process rather than an intellectual one. It is feeling rather than thinking. While the thinking center and the emotional center of the mind are not separate, they are two distinct functions operating from different levels of the self. The thinking process is centered in the cerebral cortex zone of the brain, while the emotional process resides in the cerebellum area, an older, more primitive level of the brain.

It is important for you to understand these two distinct functions, for it is a fallacy to believe that your thinking and feeling are working in tandem. Many times your feelings may run in an opposite direction to the conscious intent of your thoughts. In such a case, you are much like a car with a broken steering wheel. You may think you are headed in one direction, but your feelings are carrying you elsewhere.

To pursue this illustration, the conscious, intellectual self is like the operator of a car. The car itself is the emotional center, the feeling self. Too often the intellectual self rides along in the car without using the steering wheel, and the emotional self rambles wherever it fancies and frequently goes out of control.

That which forms a dynamic connection between the intellectual center and the emotional center is conscious direction. You must take command of the steering wheel

122

with conscious determination. If there is a lack of conscious guidance and control over the imagination, the more primitive emotional center becomes the boss. If you exercise conscious direction, you can visualize that which is true, superior, and productive of higher experiences. If you fail to exercise control, the picture room of the mind becomes a conglomerate of half-truths, false images, unlovely patterns, and fantasies that produce undesirable and disorganized experiences.

Only through direction and discrimination will superior pictures of yourself have a chance of reaching the developing stage on the emotional level. Without new command and direction, the same undesirable images will be mechanically reproduced time and time again. A person honestly may be attempting to produce better results with higher thoughts and yet fail if his thoughts are not directed to the emotional level. The production department of the emotional center knows nothing about thoughts that remain on the unfertile intellectual level.

### How to build a new self-image

To build a new self-image, you must affirm data about yourself that may, at the moment, appear to be untrue. But remember, you are not lying to yourself when you see a new image. You are simply negating the lies you have been telling yourself for too long. You are simply canceling the un-you and building a concept of the real you.

You do not have to tolerate the status quo of the self. Life is not static. It is dynamic—ever moving, ever changing, ever evolving. To give an ancient phrase new meaning, "*It* came to pass." Energy is dynamic. It passes constantly into new forms and arrangements. No one is more aware of this than the physicist who sees in such processes as combustion and oxidation that "It came to pass." Matter is here to pass into new forms. Nothing is consumed or destroyed. It simply changes form.

Just as the scientist split the atom and reorganized the energy that resulted into a new arrangement of matter, so you can take the dynamic, flowing energy of the self and redirect it to new ends.

## Laying the ghost of your old self-image

Why do forms that "came to pass" fail to pass? Why do experiences persist? They persist because of the life you give them. Remember William James's statement that "my experience is what I agree to attend to." [3]

This agreement consists of the attention that you give to a thing. It is intensified by imagination. It is sustained by visualization. It thrives on emotional recognition. It is prolonged by memory. Circumstances are held to you by these cohering elements. That which you endow with more of these cohesive elements will be more alive. That which you endow with less will be less vigorous. The more attention, concern, emotionalism, and interest you show in a particular phase of your life, the stronger it will be. But when you let your attention wane, lose interest, and become unemotional about it, you will find it fading as a factor in your experience.

STEPS IN RIDDING YOURSELF OF THE
GHOSTS OF OLD EXPERIENCES

If you are tired of an old experience of worry, failure, inadequacy or defeat, and you would like to forget the corpse—you would like to lay the ghost—what prevents you? Something holds it to you. It is the cohesive elements of memory, emotion, imagination, recognition, and attention that prevent an experience pattern from passing as it should into the limbo of yesterday. Every time you recall an old experience that should be dead—an old hurt, an old defeat—you give it a shot of life. If you make the mistake of feeding it with imagination, it will arise from its death bed and follow you into the future. So, to build a new self-image, take these steps to lay the ghost of old experiences:

1. Don't limit your view of life by what has gone before. The only power that exists in the circumstances you now find around you is the power you put there by your interest, emotion, and attention. Today is a sparkling

new day. The only impression it bears of what has gone before is the view you bring to it. Change your view, and circumstances around you will change.

**2.** Turn entirely away from any circumstances that appear unpleasant. Turn your attention, emotions, and imagination toward new causes and ignore effects that should be deceased. This is not putting your head in the sand. It is dealing properly with things that do not deserve to be revived with your attention. If you wish to demonstrate joy, turn entirely away from sorrow. You will never find wealth in the contemplation of impoverishment. You will never find love by dwelling in the tent of the lonely.

**3.** Practice the art of mental picturing. See yourself as you want to be. Don't pay court to what you do not wish to experience. Courtship leads to marriage. Look only at what you want. Contemplate your enjoyment of it. Visualize yourself possessing it. What new qualities do you wish to demonstrate? What kind of house do you want to live in five years from now? What income do you desire for your self two years from now? Your new self and your new life begin in the "now" of your visualizing. Picture yourself as possessing this new life now.

**4.** Practice rehearsing the role that embodies your new goals. Throw yourself into the part as an actor might who is rehearsing for the greatest role of his career. Past experience may have repeatedly cast you in an undesirable part. You may feel typed. Carol did. She had her role

With the brush of visualization, I paint a new concept of a superior me on the canvas of today. This new image cancels out all previous inadequate scribbles. I breathe life into it by imbuing it with the energy of my attention, emotions, and imagination. I make the image a walking-talking picture of the superior person I potentially am.

*Mental Data Processing Card No. 12*

as an unattractive person down pat. But she learned that there was no one but herself to say that she must continue to play that part, and she began rehearsing a new role. So can you! No one is forced to keep playing a Tobacco Road role. You are free to build your own Shangri-La.

5. Use Mental Data-Processing Card No. 12 to apply the art of visualization in the creation of a superior self-image:

## CHAPTER SUMMARY OF POINTS TO PONDER

1. Imagination is a unique factor that distinguishes man from the lower orders of life. With its magic, man can produce a life different from any he has ever known with mental cybernetics power.

2. Of the four basic faculties of man's mind—reflection, reason, memory, and imagination—the development of imagination is the most vital to creative success in life.

3. Imagination not only enables man to form a new synthesis of ideas from old experiences, but it empowers him to tap the endless and unborn potentials of universal mind.

4. Put your imagination to work now in making a new mental movie of life as you want it to be. Don't keep viewing the old rerun created by yesterday's limited imagination.

5. Don't confuse the picture taker with the picture taken. You, as the picture producer, are always greater than your production. You have conceived it, and you can rewrite it to your heart's desire.

6. The image you have built of yourself through imagination has become a walking-talking picture of you. It is the un-you. You cannot hide it, but you can change it into a superior image.

7. Use visualization to court this new, superior image of yourself. In your mind's eye, see the qualities of your choice belonging to you. Replace the un-you with pictures of the real you.

8. Visualization is an emotional process, not an intellectual one. You must not only put thinking into the image you wish to create; you must put feeling into it as well.

9. Remember, you are not lying to yourself when you visualize a new image. You are simply cancelling the lies you have told yourself for too long. You are giving the superior self a chance to express.

10. You will experience that thing to which you give your attention. Therefore, you can lay the ghosts of undesirable images by withdrawing your attention from them and directing your energy, emotions, interest, and imagination toward the new you.

# CHAPTER
# SEVEN

## Mental Cybernetics
## in Data-Processing
## Desires into Realities

In the folklore of the hills, a tale is told of old Zeke and his wife Sarah sitting on the porch of their mountain cabin. Zeke's rocker faced the wooded hill at the back of the property, while Sarah's faced the road. They rocked back and forth as the hours droned on in uneventful monotony. The silence at last was broken as Sarah slowly intoned, "Procession passing along the road, Pa. Lots of people all dressed up. Some are carrying banjoes and guitars. What do you suppose it is?"

"Don't rightly know, Ma," came Zeke's studied reply. "Shore wish I was turned in that direction! Shore'd like to see it!"

How many people are like Zeke? How many are turned in the wrong direction? How many have their minds turned toward dull, petty, mediocre preoccupations while a procession of grandeur and beauty passes by behind their backs? These are the people whose point of view is static. They are "sot" in their ways and will not shift to the view which could make life more exciting and productive. Although they may yearn for unfulfilled desires, they seem unwilling to turn to a more positive mental position—a more constructive viewpoint—which would change the objective scene they face.

Why are some people like Zeke? Because they have fallen victim to the data fed into their computer-like mental machinery. Remember, once thought commands have been imprinted upon the mind, automation takes over to reproduce those commands over and over again.

Thought commands are very much like keypunch cards that are stamped with specific directions. These directions activate the computer and produce corresponding results. Imagine for a moment that each individual possesses a number of keypunch cards. These are his dominant thought patterns. As long as he keeps feeding these same cards into the automatic reactor of the subconscious mind, life will drone on in the same monotonous way. The direction of his view will not change. This is the trouble that the Zekes of the world have.

How does a person acquire his dominant thought patterns? Is it by chance or by choice? Is it by the action of law or luck? Four factors impinge upon man to form such patterns. Sometimes he is aware of the imprint of these factors, but more often he is not. In any event, these factors do not operate by chance but by laws of mind as set out in this book.

## The four factors that control your thinking

Man acts from four basic determinants. The four factors that stamp their imprint on his thinking arise from these areas:

1. *The universal mind from which man springs.* Man bears the imprint of the universal urge that cradled him and brought him forth as an expression of itself. The universal, evolutionary urge to reach for ever finer and finer forms is indelibly printed in the depths of man's being.

2. *The inherited factors that affect mind and body.* Man cannot deny the genetic patterns stamped upon him that determine, to some extent, the make-up of the body chemistry, physical traits, tonal quality of the bodily systems, and cerebral functions.

3. *The habit patterns of thinking and acting that man acquires.* It is in this area that man may exercise the greatest power. Here he can either bind himself to thought patterns that keep him in bondage or he can free his mind from limitation and program his life for success.

4. *The mass factors from environment.* Also impinging upon man's thinking are the various stimuli from his environment. Here again, he can fall victim to the negative impressions that clamor for his attention or he can protect himself from the mass consciousness through the right programming of his mind.

These four determinants tend to imprint themselves upon man's dominant thinking. They become the pattern on the keypunch cards of thought that man feeds into the subconscious for processing. A definition of the word *imprint* makes its appropriateness clear in regard to the power of thought: "(1) to impress; mark by pressure; stamp; (2) to stamp or mark, as letters on paper, by means of type, plates, stamps, etc.; (3) to fix indelibly, as in memory." [1]

From universal mind, from inherited factors, from habit thinking, and from the mass consciousness, man's mind is programmed or impressed with data. His keypunch cards of thought are marked by pressure from such sources. It is these sources, and his reaction to them, that influence the direction of his desire. The pressure of habit thinking and the imprint fixed by environment may keep him from turning in a new direction to behold the grandeur and beauty of life.

However, the practice of mental cybernetics enables man to cooperate with the first of these four determinants and to change, alter, or influence the other three. It enables man to bring new pressure to bear and to change the desire commands he feeds into the reactor of the subconscious.

### How to use the dynamo of desire to break free of habit thinking

To break free of habit thinking and the pressure of mass consciousness, your desire to change must be dynamic. Strong desire is like a dynamo. Without it, very little is accomplished. With strong desire, there are virtually no assignable limits to achievement. A *dynamo* is defined as "a machine for converting mechanical energy into electrical energy, especially into direct-current electricity by electromagnetic induction." [2] Mind may be said to be a machine for the conversion of desire into action power. It is a dynamo for the direct induction of desire into demonstration. However, a desire must be imbued with energy before it can be turned into power. Desire must be dynamic to bring about change.

### The three desires basic to mankind

There are three desires basic to the human heart:

1. *The desire to belong.* This includes the desire to love and be loved, the longing for friendship, and the yearning for a sense of belonging.
2. *The desire to feel secure.* This includes the urge for the safety of home, the security of ample supply, and an assurance of the basic requirements of life.
3. *The desire to find meaning in life.* This encompasses the whole area of self-discovery, the urge to find purpose in living, to feel that you have something to contribute to life, and that you have a personal value to share with others. This embraces the longing for self-esteem, recognition, and creative fulfillment.

These three desires—to belong, to be secure, and to be of value—are basic. No individual can be truly happy without them.

If these desires are common to all, if this is what man yearns for and values, why has he so often demonstrated just the opposite? Man desires peace, but war comes. He wants prosperity, but poverty is often his lot. Mankind yearns for love, but loneliness envelopes the lives of many. If desire is a dynamo and if desire commands do activate the subconscious, why doesn't man get what he desires? The answer lies in what man has come to expect.

Unfortunately, for the vast majority, fears and doubts negate the basic desires of the heart. Negative habit thoughts and mass fears turn man's attention in the wrong

131

direction. Mass consciousness tells him to expect the worst. Although authors like Napoleon Hill have long been teaching that man can *Think and Grow Rich*,[3] man can use his creative power in reverse to think and grow poor! Expectation can cause a man to forge his life positively or negatively, depending upon the conditioning factors around him. What he comes to expect as a result of heredity, environment, and his own habit thinking, is what he demonstrates.

## Life's diary of desires

Life is very much like a diary of desires. The diary starts in early childhood and is added to continuously as man matures. The child, in his desires, is demanding, insistent, and quite possibly possesses a large measure of expectation that his desires will be fulfilled. At this stage, his list of desires is what he wants from others.

As he moves into adolescence and young adulthood, his list likely changes from what he wants of others to what he wants of himself. He speculates about a career and wonders, "Do I desire to be a doctor, a teacher, an artist, or what?" Later, his desires bring him a marriage partner and largely set the course of other desires that follow.

By the time he reaches 35 or 40, his list of desires through the years has become long; his diary is quite full. Have his desires been dynamic? Has he used desire commands to convert his wishes into action? Or have doubts and fears negated his expectations and left him with a diary of unfulfilled desires? To a great extent, he gets what he has come to expect. He gets what he bargains for!

> I bargained with life for a penny,
> And life would pay no more,
> However I begged at evening
> When I counted my scanty store.
>
> For life is a just employer,
> He gives you what you ask;
> But once you have set the wages,
> Why, you must bear the task.

I worked for a menial's hire,
Only to learn dismayed
That any wage I had asked of life,
Life would have willingly paid.[4]

What man bargains for, what he asks for and expects, is more than a single request. It must be seen against the background of years. It is man's habitual thought content that keeps asking. It is what he has accepted from his environment. It is how he has reacted to hereditary factors. It is the sum total of the data on the keypunch cards with which he has programmed his mind. This is the data with which he bargains. "Once you have set the wages, why, you must bear the task," is all too true. You must bear it until you reprogram the expectations you have forged.

*Through mental cybernetics, however, you can do just that!* You can reforge your expectations and establish a higher wage scale. This you can do through examining the instinctual and habitual asking you have done and by consciously altering or changing it with the imprinting of new desire. Of course, to expect the asking of a single day to overcome the requests of a lifetime, is demanding the impossible.

### The law of demonstration of desires

A basic law of mental cybernetics is that *a desire consistently held in mind tends to become objectified as form.* The form may be something that can be seen, as a material possession, or it may be a quality of experience, an attitude of mind, or a quality of character.

Poets, composers, inventors, architects, and creators in all fields have converted thoughts into things by definite laws that can be used by anyone. They have all turned desire into objective form. However, it must be remembered that creative artists and inventors *expect* to succeed. They expect to demonstrate their desires. Thus, to use the law of mental cybernetics effectively, you, too, must expect to see your desires manifested in form. You must raise your expectations until they match your desires.

Only conscious awareness and conscious desire can

overcome the hypnotic influence of negative expectations, doubts, and fears. The only hold that failure and poverty have is that which is exerted on the mind. The hold becomes secure when failure, squalor, and dingy surroundings become normal to the mind and what is seen day after day becomes the expected thing.

To move from desire to demonstration requires moving to higher conscious expectations—to a higher wage scale in terms of expected happiness, love, self-mastery, and supply.

### How to break the "automated expectation" image of yourself

To set wages higher and to raise expectations, the automated image you have of life must be broken. You must stop feeding the old keypunch cards of inferior desire into the automatic subconscious processor. To reprogram your mind with new desires, begin here:

*First,* awaken from the inertia of "set" desiring. Don't keep on rocking back and forth faced in the same old direction. Stimulate your imagination to greater possibility. As Elbert Hubbard remarked, "The reason men do not accomplish greater things is that they do not undertake greater things." [5]

*Second,* recognize that factors around you may be conditioning you to low expectations. As mentioned above, the child starts out with high expectations. His desires are demanding and insistent. As he grows older, his demands may be rebuffed, his insistence thwarted, and he may quickly reach the point where the feeling that "I can't have" becomes stronger than "I want." Perhaps this same deterioration of expectation has occurred in your life. If you are told by others often enough that you cannot succeed, eventually you join the chorus.

*Third,* to reactivate your desire and to reprogram your expectation of the wage life will pay, you must become aware that mental cybernetics operates as a definite law. You must leave the hazy realm of "maybe my desires will be answered" and move into the sureness that mental law works. You must trust in the automation that processes your desire once it is programmed. You must relax and let the subconscious react once your desire demand is set.

## How to build your desire demand list

As a means of sifting minor desires from major ones—and preventing important goals from becoming lost in the midst of minor needs—use a daily diary of desire to clarify your mental program. To move from desire to demonstration, consciously submit to the inner mind a desire demand list of the things you want from life.

Such a list might include material items such as a better position, a new home, a trip abroad, or intangibles such as self-confidence and poise. Make the list practical. If you need a new refrigerator or a rug for the living room, put them on your list. Don't be afraid to set the wage high. *Most people bargain with life for too little!* Figure 7–1 is a basic plan in constructing and using such a desire.

### Figure 7–1
### DAILY DIARY OF DESIRES[1]

Directions

1. Define opposite the things you really want to demonstrate. _____

2. List them in order of preference—first things first. _____

3. Eliminate desires that are incompatible. _____

4. Contemplate the list twice daily. If it is a skill you desire, see yourself using it. If it is a tangible thing you want, visualize yourself possessing it. _____

Twice each day, morning and evening, go over your daily diary of desires, letting the conscious mind focus upon each item. Affirm that the desire is even now being processed and will become objectified soon as person, place, or thing. Let the conscious mind dwell upon each desire for a full minute before passing on to the next desire demand. In the morning, contemplate each item. Then, release it to the action of the subconscious mind until you review your desire diary just before retiring for the night.

## BENEFITS IN KEEPING A DESIRE DIARY LIST

Making such a desire diary list will have these practical effects:

1. It will help to clarify in your mind what it is that you really want. Possibly, for the first time, you will spell out in a definite way things you may have wanted but never before defined.
2. It will establish priority in regard to the things you desire from life. For many people, desires play leapfrog one with another. First one desire is on top, and a few minutes later another desire demands attention. Such indecision and confusion delay your demonstration.
3. It will avoid a haziness of desire which dissipates mental force that could be used in the achievement of definite goals. Haziness of desire is one of the major power leaks of the mind. Fuzzy thinking can only beget fuzzy conditions.
4. In sifting minor desires from major ones, you will achieve a feeling of importance and urgency never before experienced. It will give you the feeling of one who is on the move. You will sense that your life has purpose and meaning. You will feel that a capable, knowing captain is at the helm.
5. It will help you to develop the power of concentration as each desire is held in mind for a full minute. In the beginning, your mind may be prone to wander. Bring it back to your desire demand firmly, but without tension.
6. It will strengthen your faith in the law of mind as you see your desires moving toward demonstrable results. As thoughts become things—as desires become demonstrations—it will stir in you the magic of gratitude. Give thanks as you see

desires moving into the good for which you have longed, for gratitude primes the pump of demonstration.

7. Use Mental Data Processing Card No. 13 to help you meditate on your daily diary of desires —your desire demand list—giving special emphasis to the feeling that these desires are being processed *now* for you.

My attention now focuses on one item from my desire demand list [identify it]. In my mind, that desire takes on definite shape and form. Its image is printed in technicolor detail upon the keypunch card of thought. As a mental reality, its possession thrills me now! I give thanks for it and release it to creative mind for processing.

*Mental Data Processing Card No. 13*

## How to program specific desires

"In using mental cybernetics, how specific can I be in regard to the things I want?" Frank Delry asked as he explained to me his life and his extreme dissatisfaction. Frank was a young man in his late twenties, happily married, and the father of four lovely children. He had a good job from a monetary standpoint, but it was production line work and Frank's heart belonged to the wide open spaces. City life cramped his style. This was his one and only problem.

"I've always known what I wanted," Frank continued, "and this is not for me. I love ranch life. In the city I feel hemmed in. I attended agricultural college, and I feel that I belong on a ranch. Fortunately, I married a girl who shares my desire to live in the country. I'd like to find a ranch that needed a foreman where I might be able to run a few head of cattle, have my own horse, and enjoy the feeling of freedom again. But can I be this

137

specific when programming a desire into the computer of the subconscious?"

"How specific do you want to be?" I asked.

"Well, I can just see the type of ranch where I'd like to live. I can mentally picture the kind of job I'd like to be doing. But would I be limiting my chances too much to pick the area in which I'd like to find such a ranch?"

"What area do you have in mind?" I asked.

"Well," he said, becoming more animated, "let's think of a line running from Kingman, Arizona, down to Phoenix. I'd like to locate on land extending from that line east for 500 miles."

Noting the smile on my face, he hesitated. "I guess I'm being too specific."

"Well," I replied, "you have narrowed it down to a very definitive area, but if this location is top priority for you, let's give it a try."

I asked Frank to come to my office each week, and we had a session together on the laws of mental cybernetics. Using desire as the dynamo, he visualized the new life he planned. He mentally "saw" himself on his beloved ranch. His visualizing and imagining helped to subjectify his desire as an image in the subconscious. He programmed his specific desire into the subconscious and set the creative inner mind in motion.

Secondly, I asked Frank to do the muscular—to do everything of a physical nature that would help him in the realization of his dream, such as putting his name in farm journals, checking the advertisements, and answering all leads regardless of whether they seemed ideal or not. He promised to follow through with this program without fail.

For about three months very little of an objective nature happened. In spite of the passage of time, his faith remained high. He understood that the law of mental cybernetics had been set in motion. He understood that plans and opportunities had to mature on the invisible mental level before visible results could be seen.

Then one day Frank came to my study in a deeply meditative mood. I could see that he wanted to talk— that he had decisions to make. Frank had received an

138

offer, but it was not for his chosen area. The offer had come from the owner of a ranch in northern Nevada.

"Should I respond? Maybe even consider going to northern Nevada? It is an attractive offer. Many factors seem so right—a house of our own, full authority as foreman, and the freedom I desire. Should I consider this an answer to my desire command?"

Knowing that anxiety and tension can interfere with the demonstration of desires, I encouraged Frank to relax in regard to the matter. "It can't hurt to reply. Find out more about the offer," I said. It was almost four months since Frank had first entered my office. He was becoming tense and needed something concrete to do.

"Just say enough to keep the door open," I advised, "and then relax and release the matter. In the meantime we'll program a guidance request into the subconscious. If the place is right, the job will be yours. If it is not the answer to your desire command, the door to it will close."

A few days later, with another letter from the Nevada rancher and the opportunity this offer seemed to afford, Frank was on the verge of accepting. He was completing arrangements, winding up his business, and making serious plans to leave for Nevada. Just when his future seemed all settled, Frank bounded into my study with a new offer he had just received. His radiant smile spoke for itself. I didn't have to guess the area from which this new contact came—I knew!

It was over a year before I heard from Frank again. He was now foreman of a ranch just southeast of Prescott, Arizona. From the sound of his letter, he was supremely happy. He had demonstrated his desire.

### How demonstration corresponds with desire

There are those who might say that the demonstration of Frank Delry was just coincidence—that it just happened that way. However, the word *coincidence* explains nothing. It is one of those meaningless words that is used to avoid explanation. The dictionary helps some. It defines coincidence as "correspondence." Thus, it might be said that there was a correspondence between Frank's desire and the job he demonstrated. How does such a correspondence come about? The science of mental cybernetics gives the answer. Demonstration corresponds with desire —or coincidence with an internal state of mind—because desire activates a mental law that guides the individual along the path from thought to thing, when certain requirements are fulfilled.

## FOUR DYNAMIC FACTORS FOR DEMONSTRATION OF DESIRES

What are these requirements? Four dynamic factors are involved in successful demonstrations such as that made by Frank Delry.

*First,* Frank knew what he wanted. He was clear and definite about the life he desired.

*Second,* knowing what he wanted, he decided to do something about it—i.e., he acted upon his desires; he did the muscular; he used the laws of mental cybernetics.

*Third,* he persisted in the decision that he made until it became an objective fact of experience.

*Fourth,* he had faith that life would honor his desire.

*Frank used the mental cybernetics techniques that you can use to demonstrate your heartfelt desires.* To program your mind for success, be clear and consistent in your aspirations. Next, do the muscular, prepare yourself, and build the skills that will qualify you for the demonstration you wish to make. Then persist in that desire. Pursue it with determination. Be true to your aspirations in everything you do and say and think. Fourth, draw your persistence and determination from faith in something greater than you are. When you program your mind for success, you are tapping the creative power of subconscious mind—not only your mind but the universal mind from which you spring.

The creative mind within you derives from the creative principle that brought forth all things. When you place a desire command in the subconscious for processing, you set in motion that mind which has infinite "know-how." Latent in its creative nature are all the known and unknown laws of chemistry, physics, biology, telepathy, telekinetics, and other powers ad infinitum. The scope of the subconscious mind is unlimited, for its source is the creative principle underlying the universe. When you use your creative mind, you are using something greater than yourself.

## Secrets of subconscious automation

What the conscious mind initiates, the subconscious mind must implement. The ingenuity of the subconscious in working out the answers to conscious desires is remarkable and sometimes quite awesome. Remember, the subconscious mind obeys desire commands, but it does not monitor them and sort the wise from the unwise. It is the conscious mind that must monitor desires and keep them constructive. The subconscious accepts commands, be they positive or negative, and automation takes over to manifest those commands.

For example, in the insatiable longing of the gambler or alcoholic is found a desire so strong that the subconscious mind engineers the individual into remarkable opportunities to fulfill his craving. Unexpected invitations to drink and "accidental" chances to gamble will come about in ways not planned by the conscious mind. By the same token, keen positive desires will automate the subconscious mind toward opportunities of fulfillment of which the conscious intellect never even dreamed.

As soon as a desire becomes dominant, the subconscious mind begins to work out the practical details of its fulfillment. This deeper level of mind is infinitely creative but not selective. It takes the data supplied by conscious choice—or by thoughtless acquiescence—and guides the self toward demonstration. This guidance may take the form of meeting someone or of avoiding someone. It may maneuver one into taking a trip, visiting a friend, making a needed contact, or meeting someone by "accident." And all of this happens according to a law of mind—a science of mind.

## Choice is a responsibility of conscious mind

Because the subconscious mind will process any desire command programmed into it, the awesome responsibility of formulating constructive commands becomes apparent.

141

From the moment when man evolved to an upright position and, aware of himself, was able to say, "I am," the responsibility of decision-making became a function of his conscious mind.

This is not to say that other decision-making factors do not impinge upon man. There are certain things he cannot consciously choose. He cannot select his sex, nor the race or culture into which he is born. As conscious choice, he cannot select who his family is, what its religious or moral convictions are, or the time of his birth. Certain states of being into which man is thrust are of collective creation such as the economic and political conditions under which he comes into the world and the mass consciousness of the times.

But, in spite of all of these factors that seem to be pre-selected for man, he still has a degree of choice in regard to them. He can choose to react affirmatively or negatively. He can choose to reject the status in which he finds himself and to climb to new heights. He can decide to turn adversity into the challenge to grow, to mature, and to seek new opportunity.

Thus, although the individual's life is interwoven with the life of mankind and the stage seems set in regard to his sex, color, and ethnic background, there is no reason for saying, "There is nothing I can do." Your freedom of choice rests in your awareness of being. You are a point of life expressing itself at the level of your acceptance. Your experiences are the projection of your thought —what you have accepted, what you have initiated, and what you have acquiesced to. The freedom to choose is within you. Your happiness, your security, your attainments, are within you—all within that infinite *you* that you are.

### What to include in your desire

In programming desire commands into creative mind, the choice of wise desires becomes a prime consideration. Your freedom to choose places you in a position of great responsibility. Your bigness of thought will determine whether you select a goal that focuses on primary good or whether you work separately on a series of lesser desires. Before formulating your desires, consider the story told of Solomon when he became king. He asked not for riches, wealth, honor, or long life. His request was simply, "Give me now wisdom and knowledge." [6] Although his request was simple, it was not small. In its fulfillment all the lesser things it included were added unto him, and he was granted riches and wealth and honor the like of which none of the kings before him or after him enjoyed.

Many individuals strain unnecessarily for particular things, whereas, if they had a dynamic desire that was big enough, it would include the smaller particulars. Big desires encompass lesser good. It is not that lesser things are not desirable but that they will come naturally as by-products of greater things. Thus, when your goal is one of greatness in terms of service, understanding, creativeness, and self-mastery, its fulfillment will draw to you all that is required for that goal. This is the inclusion principle inherent in mental cybernetics that provides: *A desire of primary magnitude includes in its manifestation the secondary good natural to it.*

A second aspect of the inclusion principle that should be considered by you before a desire command is programmed into the subconscious calls attention to the ramifications that accompany a desire. Stop and analyze the ramifications natural to the goal you are now entertaining. For example, should you want to be a musician, do you also want the long hours of practice required? Should you want to be a politician, are you willing to accept the rough and tumble game of the political arena? Are you willing to have your private life become public domain? Should you want to be a millionaire, are you ready to handle the responsibility that goes with such wealth? Figuratively speaking, the person who yearns to be a mechanic or a prize fighter is sometimes unwilling to get greasy or be punched in the nose.

To look longingly at some line of work and say, "Wouldn't that be nice!" is not meaningful unless you are willing to include in your desire the long hours of study and practice that are required for the manifestation of that desire. Your desire is not realistic until you in-

143

clude the essentials of study, work, persistence, and dedication.

### How to formulate a realistic desire

Formulate a realistic desire—one that means so much to you that you are willing to accept the self-improvement it requires. Don't let your limit of normal desire restrict your life to mediocrity. Your life will move in the direction of your basic goal. If you have kept your desire on a short leash, let it out and expand your expectations!

The creative, subconscious level of your mind is like a computer. It acts upon the mental and emotional data that you feed it. As you go about your work, as you think, plan, read, or converse with others, this data is being processed into experience for you.

*Data* is the plural of *datum,* which is defined as: "1. Something given or admitted as a fact on which an inference is based; 2. Something actual or assumed, used as a basis of reckoning." [7] What data, actual or assumed, sways your thinking? What desires have you admitted today to be true for you? What goals have you assumed to be normal for you in spite of latent abilities? What have you inferred as fact, regarding your standard of achievement? What data—true, half-true, and false— have you programmed into your mind today? Examine it. Throw out the half-true and the false. And reprogram your mind with the realistic desire demands you listed in your Daily Diary of Desires. Then use these three D's of demonstration to bring those desires to fulfillment.

### The dynamic three "D's" of demonstration of your desires

Desire, decision, determination—these are the mental factors that lead to self-fulfillment. Desire is the motivating force in life. But from desire must spring the decision to act, and accompanying the decision to act must be determination. You can't spend your life desiring. Decide to put your desires to work and, then, persist in them. Without decision, desire will not accomplish what it is capable of doing. William James once said, "Think it

144

over, yes, but don't dilly-dally until someone else has thought it over, worked it out and put it over." [8]

Desire greatly, choose decisively, and act with determination. Then relax. Let go and let your desire be processed. To quote James again, "When once a decision is reached and execution is the order of the day, dismiss absolutely all responsibility and care about the outcome." [9] It is imperative that you let the subconscious mind consummate the desire command you have given it. Do not cancel your command with doubts, worry, anxiety, or countercommands.

## Rules for action for applying the three D's of demonstration

*First,* don't dilly-dally, but do take time to choose. Decisions that may have a bearing on your future happiness should not be made in haste or on the rebound. Don't let momentary irritations settle a question about changing jobs or selecting a life partner. Your decision should be a conscious act, not an unconscious reaction.

*Second,* seek the advice of others. Successful people in every field analyze the advice of others whose opinions and judgment they value. However, the final decision you make must be your own, and you must take the responsibility for it. Maintain the integrity of your own mind, and don't be unduly swayed by those who "know what is best for you."

*Third,* free yourself of any negative hold from decisions of yesterday. Perhaps you made a mistake. Perhaps it would be easy to bemoan lost chances and opportunities. You could whip yourself mercilessly, but to what avail? Maybe choices you made in the past were wrong from every apparent standpoint, but they were necessary for you at that level because you didn't know better. Forgive yourself. If you had known better, you would have done better! The quip that good judgment comes from poor judgment is not without merit. Your decisions of yesterday added to your mental and emotional growth and brought you to this point. Now you do know better and can choose better.

nation. Then relax. Let go and let your desire be pro-

*Fourth,* once you have evaluated your choice consciously and decided upon it, persist in your decision. Of course, you want to feel that your choice is right. If there is any doubt, program a guidance request into the subconscious. Simply add to your desire command the provision that if its fulfillment is for your greatest good, it will be blocked.

*Finally,* as a fifth action rule, work daily with your Diary of Desires and Mental Data Processing Card No. 14, persisting until your desires become a new motivating force in your life.

*Mental Data Processing Card No. 14*

## CHAPTER SUMMARY OF POINTS TO PONDER

1. The man who is "sot" in his ways has let himself be victimized by his own habit thoughts. And as long as he keeps feeding these same thought patterns into the automatic reactor of subconscious mind, he will plod on in the same old rut.

2. To break free of habit-thinking, man must generate an impelling desire to change. A strong desire acts like a dynamo. It supplies the energy necessary to reverse the direction of life.

3. Combined with the desire to change must be the *expectation* that new accomplishments can really be achieved. To hope for the best and *expect* the worst is like trying to illumine a room by turning off the light.

146

4. What man bargains for—what he expects—is dictated by the thought content that has been accumulating in his subconscious for years. Negative expectations, subconscious fears, doubts, and self-depreciation cannot be cancelled out with *one attempt* at positive thinking.

5. To set higher wages and build positive expectations, man must practice the daily and persistent reforming of his mental image of himself, with the use of some device like a Daily Diary of Desire.

6. To move persistently from desire to demonstration, man must utilize the faith that comes from knowing that there is something greater than himself. When he places a thought command in the subconscious, he sets in motion a greater, creative mind that has infinite "know-how."

7. In defining desire, man needs to be specific enough to clarify the results he wishes. However, he need not strain over ways and means, for once a desire becomes dominant, the subconscious begins to work out the practical details of fulfillment.

8. In choosing his demonstration, man should set a goal big enough to include lesser desires. Many a secondary goal is manifested as a by-product of a primary desire.

9. Man's normal level of expectation acts like a leash that keeps him tethered to ordinary demonstrations. Normal desires must give way to supernormal expectations!

10. To reinforce the mental work man does when using the laws of mental cybernetics, he must also do the muscular. He must take steps on the physical plane of action to prepare the way for the demonstration of his desire.

# CHAPTER
# EIGHT

## *How to Guard*
## *Yourself Against*
## *Hypnotic Influences*

"Gaze into my eyes. Keep looking . . . keep looking," intones the villain as he stares with fixed gaze upon the beautiful young maiden. "You are now in my power! You are in love with me, my dear. You will remember nothing else—only that you love me." The curtain falls as the audience anxiously ponders the fate of the innocent maiden.

The next act shows the beautiful young damsel in a stormy scene with the boy she had planned to marry since childhood. She breaks the engagement and throws his ring at his feet. The boy pleads desperately with his sweetheart to reconsider, but in vain. She is determined to marry the villain, with whom she believes herself to be in love.

The boy persists. He tells his lady fair that the villain doesn't love her and wants her only for her money. But the young maiden will not listen. She opens the door and rejects the boy she had loved. Sadly he walks out of her life.

The final act of the gaslight melodrama finds the villain and young damsel before the preacher. The blissful knot is about to be tied when the maiden comes to her senses and flees from the room. The closing scene shows the girl and her real love walking hand in hand into the sunset. Everything ends happily. The audience leaves the theater with a sigh of relief that the hypnotic spell was broken just in time.

148

In legend and folklore, great credence has been given to the power of the "hypnotic eye." He who possessed it was feared and held in awe. In the early days of hypnotism, instruction in the practice of the art placed importance upon the fixity of the gaze. It was the eye of the hypnotist that was credited with spellbinding powers. In vintage movies, the stereotyped hypnotist is usually depicted with dark, penetrating eyes that cast their magic spell as the camera moves toward them in a dramatic close-up.

However, as hypnotism evolved into a science, it was recognized that the function of the set gaze was only to bring the mind of the subject to a focal point of attention. Any object may serve that purpose. A glass ball called the "magic eye" is effective. A ball or a coin used as a pendulum now serves as the traditional object of concentration.

The interesting thing to note is that the hypnotized subject does fall victim to the thing upon which he fixes his attention—be it the eye of the hypnotist or the swinging glass eye of the pendulum. A "spell" is cast by the object on which the subject concentrates. How very much like life itself this is! That to which man gives his attention through the years tends to cast a spell on him. The things that he sees and concentrates upon have a hypnotic influence on him, making him oblivious to greater potentialities around him.

Imagine for a moment that there are hypnotic eyes around you, eyes that meet your eyes and hold your attention. Your gaze becomes riveted on them and you see nothing else. As you concentrate more and more on them, it is almost as if you are seeing life through the eyes of someone else.

Don't laugh at such fancy, for actually, it is not fancy but fact. Hypnotic eyes do surround you. They exist as the influences that have helped to form and shape your thinking. They are the exterior forces that have helped to program your mind. Think back and you will realize that you have come to see life through the eyes of others.

First, you saw life through the perceptive level of your

parents, through the attitudes of other members of your family, and through the environmental atmosphere surrounding you.

Second, you view life through the eyes of society—through its educational program, its moral standards, and its traditional values and purposes.

Third, you see life with eyes tempered with tolerance or inflamed with the prejudice of racially acquired attitudes.

Fourth, you envision life through the maturity level of the philosophical and religious concepts around you.

As you consider the above list, doubtlessly you will be able to identify factors in it that have woven their spell in your life. To some extent, everyone falls under the hypnotic influence of the eyes of dominant people and conditions around them. It can hardly be avoided in a society built on close proximity of dwelling and interdependence. A real danger lurks in such influences when they become unduly strong. Like the hypnotized subject, you can become oblivious to reality when your attention is warped in the wrong direction and you see through eyes that are prejudiced or immature. Like the fair young maiden, you may become beguiled and misguided if you gaze too long in the villain's direction.

The villain in man's life may be environmental deprivation that lures him into a poverty consciousness. It may be personal habits such as excessive drinking or smoking that have cast their spell upon him and hold him in bondage. It may be the lack of a high-school diploma that beguiles him into a feeling of inadequacy. It may be religious convictions that have hypnotized him into thinking that he is an unworthy worm of the dust. From every side—from family, environment, and society—powerful suggestive forces enter man's mind and cause him to fall asleep to the true potentialities within him.

## Your daytime sleep

The purpose of life is to awaken—to become consciously aware of the real self within and of the nature of life. To fulfill this purpose man does not need to manipulate the universe or attempt to make it go his way.

150

He *does* need to learn the way of life and align himse[lf] with that way. But his problem—and his only problem—is that he is asleep. This truth is not easy to accept, bu[t] its acceptance is the beginning of wisdom.

The person who is taking a nap doesn't put up too much resistance when told it is time to get up. He'll stir himself and perhaps respond with a grumble or two. But the person who is told to wake up mentally responds with a burst of indignation and a dark, surly look. No one likes to think that he is asleep and missing out on a better life. Have you, however, ever considered the possibility that you spend your nights sleeping and your days dreaming of being awake?

This dream of being awake—this daytime sleep—helps explain some of the incongruities you find around you. Do you believe that the conditions of the world would be what they are if mankind were awake? Would man constantly be going to war with other men if he were fully awakened? As strange and as paradoxical as it may seem, mankind has awakened only to the degree that it is aware of the pain of being asleep.

What of your life? Do you often hurt yourself, humiliate yourself, degrade yourself, or say things that show you hold yourself in low esteem? Would you do things that deny you the best in life, would you fail to appropriate the happiness that belongs to you, would you belittle your ability and deny yourself the abundance that belongs to you, if you were not asleep? During your nighttime sleep, you are physically restored and your body is refreshed. But, during your daytime sleep, you hurt yourself, say unkind things about yourself, impoverish yourself and make yourself and others unhappy. If this isn't sleep, what's your excuse?

What hypnotic eyes have usurped your attention? What has beguiled you into thinking that you must hurt yourself with self-condemnation? What has misled you to accept limitation as your lot? What has hypnotized you into hurting others with ridicule and ill temper? Until you awaken mentally, you will not be able to identify the factors that have hypnotized you and hold you in your present state of "daytime sleep."

Like the hypnotized young damsel in the gaslight melodrama who was unconscious of the suggestion that held her spellbound, man allows much of his living to be motivated by unconscious, unreasoned suggestions. These unconscious suggestions have been programmed into his mind from the hypnotic influences of dominant people and conditions around him. If told to awaken from these unconscious influences, man is apt to protest, "But, I'm not hypnotized! I am awake! I am conscious!" Regrettably, the conscious state that man thinks he enjoys is all too often a passive consciousness that acquiesces to influences around it and is, in truth, a daytime sleep.

Many centuries ago, Paul described this state of awareness when he said, "I do not understand my own actions, for I do not do what I want, but I do the very thing I hate." [1] This is a state of unconscious, mechanical control rather than of conscious action. It is the hypnotic state.

## Post-hypnotic suggestion

James T. Fisher, a psychiatrist who for over 50 years listened to the problems of thousands of people, speaks of some of the unconscious influences motivating man in his book, *A Few Buttons Missing*. In the volume, he tells of the first hypnotic demonstration he witnessed as a young intern. With variations, the phenomenon he describes has been repeated again and again and is now a classic demonstration of the suggestibility of mind.

As the interns watched, the hypnotist put a young man into a trance condition. Then, Fisher reports:

> This young man was informed that upon awakening he would be unable to see a large desk until after he had actually bumped into it. Upon being brought out of the trance, he gave every appearance of being normal and rational. And yet when asked to name the items of furniture in the room, he named everything except the large desk. When he was asked to walk to the front of the room, he bumped into the desk while making no attempt to avoid it or to shield himself from the blow. This was a demonstra-

tion of that highly peculiar situation known as the post-hypnotic suggestion.[2]

Hypnotic demonstrations such as this, conducted under scientific scrutiny, reveal several vital factors about the nature of conscious and subconscious mind. First, it becomes clear that man does have a mind that possesses dual functions—the conscious and subconscious—and that while the conscious is asleep or oblivious to reality, the subconscious mind carries on with full creativeness.

It is the ordinary function of the conscious mind to give all voluntary commands—be they in the form of choices, decisions, plans, desires, dynamic aspirations or passive acceptances. It is the function of the subconscious to act on such choices—be they simple directions like pressing a light switch or involved ones like flying an airplane. In acting upon conscious choices, the subconscious performs incredible feats of creativeness. It can turn a ham sandwich into energy or fingernails. It can be programmed to retain and reproduce a folk tune or a piano concerto. It can be tapped for inspiration and inventive know-how. The reach of the subconscious extends into telepathy, telekinetics, and powers beyond the imagination.

But, with all its powers, the subconscious is the servant of the conscious. It is suggestible. It unquestioningly accepts the suggestions of the conscious and acts upon them. It does not judge a command as wise or unwise, unless directed to do so. It simply obeys whatever the conscious mind initiates. Conscious mind is the initiator and subconscious mind is the performer. Conscious mind is the programmer and the subconscious is the programmed. However, when the conscious mind submits to hypnotic influence, then the conscious mind of an outsider becomes the programmer. In a hypnotic demonstration, the hypnotist is the outsider. In the "daytime sleep" in which man often walks, dominant influences around him become the outside forces that program his subconscious mind. It is the hold of such outside forces that man must break if he is to become fully conscious, fully awake, and able to reprogram his mind for success.

To reprogram the mind, it is essential to understand these factors about the nature of the subconscious:

1. The hypnotic state is the normal operative level of the subconscious mind—its performance always is governed by suggestion. It may be current suggestions from the conscious mind, old images programmed and stored in the subconscious, or suggestions from dominant outside influences.
2. The subconscious is receptive in nature. Therefore, it is constantly amenable to impressions from all sources. It is the duty of the conscious mind to screen these sources and to be alert to the consequences of impressions seeking entrance.
3. The subconscious mind is infinitely creative, possessing a know-how of accomplishment that is unlimited.

### How to be your own hypnotist

Considering the first point, that the normal operative level of the subconscious is the hypnotic state, to what extent is your life being lived from that hypnotized level? Would you guess that you are in conscious control 90 percent of the day? Psychologists who have made a special study of mental development feel that very few people use more than 10 percent of their conscious mental potential. Conscious awareness is only at an embryonic state of unfoldment. It may be more accurate to guess that people generally function 99 percent subconsciously to 1 percent consciously. A few may possibly function 95 to 5 percent, with a rare number of enlightened people functioning at a 90 to 10 percent ratio.

The average person who operates 99 percent at the subconscious level is living under what might be called "saturation" hypnosis. What he does is what he has been told to do—told by parents, by the forces of society, by dictates of environment, and by dominant conditions in

154

his life. His experience will be largely what others have told him his experience should be.

Considering the second point, that the subconscious is receptive and therefore is constantly amenable to all impressions, to what extent can you screen those impressions and protect the subconscious from negative programming? Negative impressions may originate in your own conscious mind. They may originate from what you read, from what you listen to on radio and television, and from the environment around you.

For example, the person born in a slum environment may come to see life through the eye of poverty. Thus, poverty is the hypnotic eye that holds him to its suggestion. Or another person may grow up in a family where constant bickering is the order of the day. He may come to see the world with an antagonistic eye that beguiles him into unhappiness in marital and social relationships. Chronic ill health is another powerful suggestion that may dominate the life of the individual. There is no limit to the range of sorrows created by looking at life through eyes that see only problems, problems that hold one to their suggestion.

To screen out negative impressions regardless of where they originate—in your environment or in your own personality—you can make deliberate use of the post-hypnotic suggestion phenomenon. To use it, assume the role of hypnotist. Assert your right to direct the subconscious. Claim full conscious authority over your subconscious mind and then command it to screen out negative suggestions that you may henceforth encounter. Direct that you be led around any obstacles that would block your good, even if you are unaware of them. Then, relax and release the command, knowing it will operate as a post-effect in your life.

### Independence from hypnotic eyes

Who told you to walk into poverty, into loneliness, into illness, into unhappiness and self-denial? What influence in your life stamped you with post-hypnotic suggestions you are now carrying out? For the most part, you are as unaware of such influences as the young man who walked into the desk. All the interns in the room could see the desk except the boy under the influence of the suggestion. In like manner, another person looking at you might be able to say, "Can't you see where you are going? Can't you see that you are walking right into trouble? You are walking into loneliness—you are walking into unhappiness with your eyes wide open!"

Yes, your eyes may be wide open physically, but the eyes of the mind are not aware. They are closed. You are hypnotized. The suggestions that you are obeying may not be much different from those that a professional hypnotist could provide. If he put you in a trance and told you to crow like a rooster, you would crow. But, what is more important, you may have told yourself to cry about your lot in life, and you have been crying ever since. Again, if a hypnotist told you that you were chained to a chair and couldn't get away, in what way would this differ from a parent, teacher, or employer in your youth telling you that you would never amount to much? Who told you to choose the path of failure? Who told you to walk down the street of regret or resentment? Who told you to spend your days circling the swamp of despair? To what hypnotic eyes have you submitted? Spurn them now and submit no longer!

## How to break the hypnotic set

The influences referred to in this chapter as "hypnotic" may also be defined as the programmed set of your mind of which you are unaware. To discover that hypnotic set and change it, follow these steps:

1. Realize that factors in your life to which you have become conditioned have some hypnotic hold on you, some influence of which you are unaware. The salary level to which you are conditioned holds you in its spell unless you take positive action to raise it. The experience level to which you are accustomed holds you within its limited perimeter unless you take concrete steps to expand it. Nothing holds you to the street you are now traveling except habit. At any time you choose, you may take a different course in life. To walk the same street too long is to submit to its hypnotic spell.

**2.** Bring your actions more and more under conscious scrutiny. Try to improve the ratio of conscious and unconscious functioning. Stop frequently to consciously question your reasons for doing as you do and thinking as you do. Don't let your day be a series of automatic stimulus-response experiences. Step back from yourself and observe your motives from time to time, and reject those that do not fit into the self-image you wish. Spurn impulses that would mislead you, as the young damsel spurned the villain at the altar.

**3.** Regulate what is programmed into the suggestible subconscious by constantly giving yourself a post-hypnotic suggestion. Remember, the subconscious does not judge between the wise and unwise unless directed to do so. Give such direction now. Command the subconscious mind to screen out all that is not productive of your highest good from all past and future programming. Use Mental Data Processing Card No. 15 to initiate this guidance-action now.

> I now assume my rightful role as conscious director of my life. I am in full authority! With the power vested in me, I now direct my subconscious mind to screen out of my experience all that is not for my highest good and to lead me safely around all obstacles. I now relax, knowing that this command will operate as a post-effect in my life henceforth and for evermore.

*Mental Data Processing Card No. 15*

## The only thing to fear is fear itself

In 1960, a midwestern newspaper carried an article of a man who appeared at the police department one day asking for protection. He accused his wife and brother of committing murder—his murder. Upon being questioned, it was learned that no actual attempt had been made upon his life. Yet he adamantly affirmed they were killing him.

As he talked, the story which unfolded was that his wife and brother had fallen in love. It was his fear that in their desire to be together, they wanted to remove him from the scene permanently. His suspicion was fanned by the fact that his brother would also benefit financially as beneficiary of the farm where they lived jointly.

Over and over again, the man alleged that his brother and wife were killing him. When asked by the police to produce evidence they could use against the pair, the man spoke of a "hex" they had placed upon him. He asserted that as a result of the hex he was slowly dying. In his mind they were killing him and he wanted the law to protect him. Of course, the police could only smile. No overt attempt had been made upon his life. Therefore, no law that was on the statute books had been violated and no arrests could be made.

The initial reaction is to chuckle at the notion of hexes and spells in this scientific age. The logical mind consigns the practice of voodoo to former times and primitive levels. Credulity scorns the belief that one person can influence another, harm him, or bring actual death by the employment of mental power alone.

Yet the fear felt by the man who sought police protection was very real. He desperately feared the hex placed upon him. Perhaps the whole key to spells and hypnotic influence is right here—here in fear itself. Fear is a device that focuses the attention in the wrong direction. A negative preoccupation may result that is actually destructive of health and happiness.

No circumstance has the power to cast a "spell" unless a man permits it to do so. He may give that permission unwittingly by believing in a superstition. He may give that permission by accepting as true that which is false. He may give that permission by fearing something that has little basis except in his imagination.

### Can another person destroy your happiness?

Can outside influences have power over you? The only power they can have is what you give them. The person who can be hexed by voodoo believes in voodoo, and hence gives it power over him. The person who can be permanently chained to poverty believes in it, and hence gives it power over him. The person who can become a victim of inferiority believes in his inadequacy, and hence gives it power over him.

Circumstances around you upon which you concentrate (the hypnotic eyes referred to before), wield power over you only as you acquiesce to them. If those circumstances are positive and productive of good, you are programming yourself for success. If those circumstances are negative or limiting, you are chaining yourself to an influence that holds you captive. To what are you giving power?

For example, the man in the news release gave his brother and wife power over him through his fear of what they planned and what might happen. He was permitting himself to be used by suspicion and jealousy. I remember a couple who permitted themselves to be used by possessiveness.

## A CASE OF PARENTAL HYPNOSIS

Robert and Carolyn found each other in the springtime of the year and in the springtime of life. Bob was 22 and Carolyn was 19. It so happened that Bob was an only child. He was loved greatly—possessively—by his parents. They could not bear to part with him. Although they were strong and healthy, they asked their son to promise not to marry until after they were gone. They had married late in life. Now, they lived for their son, and they wanted their son to live for them.

The son gave his promise, and a courtship of 23 years ensued between Carolyn and Bob. Finally, his father passed away, and then his mother. At last Bob and Carolyn were able to marry. By this time he was 45 and Carolyn was 42.

They seemed happy, but they did not have children. They had been cheated out of those young, vigorous years together when most couples build a home and enjoy the fulfillment of rearing a family. They had let themselves be used by an outside influence that dominated their lives. By acquiescing to the hypnotic "eye" of his parents, Bob and Carolyn gave it power over them.

## Is anyone misusing your mind?

If you were asked the question, "Who's using your mind," you probably would reply, "Why, I am, of course!" But, would you be entirely correct? Are you living your life, or are you living the life another person demands of you—like Bob and Carolyn? Are you using your mind, or is your mind being used—or misused, as the case may be—by others?

Actually, the vast body of mankind today is swayed and influenced and "used" by others—even by others who have not been around in objective form for a long, long time. Their influence persists as the mass thought passed on to each new generation from those who have thought, written, spoken, and acted down through the ages. Indeed, mass thought is the great hypnotist of mankind today. Post-hypnotic suggestions, passed down through generations of time, persist in the mass mind and impel men to make blind and senseless decisions.

Each child awakens to life at birth, only to fall asleep again with those around him as the hypnotic spell of mass consciousness weaves its pattern into his thought. Mass thought forms tracks in mind, and, once a person lets his train of thought get on that track, it is difficult to get off again. A certain prejudice or conviction, once thought, tends to become habitual. Over and over, with mechanical monotony, mankind repeats fallacies that have worn deep ruts in the mass mind. Each newcomer to the human family is a potential victim of those same fallacies unless he learns that he is free to program his mind with fresh data.

## The conquest of negative complexes

It is never too late to declare your freedom from influences exerted by mass consciousness, environment, society, and domineering people around you. You can make a start by consciously examining your actions and reactions and identifying the impulses that motivate you.

You will discover motives of which you were unaware. You will find desires and memories that you wish to discard.

In the course of living, man builds a system of thoughts —some gleaned from the mass mind and some from individual experience—that become the mental complex within which he functions. If this complex or composite is positive, it results in a success consciousness. If the composite is negative, it may result in an inferiority complex, a poverty complex, an accident-prone complex, etc.

Psychologically defined, a complex is "a system of desires and memories which in disguised form exert a dominating influence upon the personality." [3] When the psychiatrist speaks of a complex, he is referring to a basic drive that has become frustrated through repression or conflicting beliefs, resulting in a distortion of personality.

Man may build up a false system of desires and memories in regard to any of the basic urges—nutritive, sexual, acquisitive, domestic, social, religious, desire for pleasure, power, etc. If that system of desires is disguised and dominates his personality, then he has a "complex" in the psychological sense.

In Freud's philosophy, most complexes arise from a frustrated sexual urge. Adler, in contrast, sees the power-drive or struggle for superiority as the primary factor that motivates man. Jung feels that man basically is seeking a balanced view of life through self-realization. Some psychologists see man as a creature motivated mainly by subconscious feelings, others see him reacting mainly to stimulus-response impulses, and still others view him as a conscious, logical being.

Actually, they have all highlighted a vital, separate facet of man's mental makeup. When those separate facets are put together as the whole man, a real grasp of his complex nature—and his complexes—emerges. Man is both a conscious and subconscious being. He does have the conscious faculty to reason logically. However, once conscious commands (his own and those to which he has submitted) have been released to the subconscious, the subconscious continues to perpetuate

161

them whether they are wise or unwise, true or false. Once a system of desires is programmed into the subconscious, it stays imbedded there as a complex until some reprogramming takes place. Complexes operate on the feeling level and not on the intellect level.

## How to dehypnotize yourself

To dehypnotize yourself from the complexes that may be operating on the feeling level and from influences that impinge upon you from your environment, society, mass consciousness, and domineering individuals around you, you must awake consciously. The hypnotized person has let himself fall asleep or become oblivious to certain truths about himself. To awaken, he must become consciously aware of these truths. You can dehypnotize yourself now by awaking to these facts:

*First,* you must see that life seeks to express by means of you. It seeks to express its freedom, its vigor, its inventiveness, its curiosity, and its creativeness through you. You are a channel for the flow of power—a power that cannot be bottled up without serious consequences to your personal happiness and sense of well being.

*Second,* awake to the fact that a disguised system of desires and memories programmed into the subconscious by the hypnotic "eyes" surrounding you—through environment, society, family prejudices, cultural preferences, and educational media—may be dominating your personality.

*Third,* assert your independence of thought. This is not to say that all of the preprogrammed thought you have accepted is wrong, but, without independent analysis, yau cannot sift from the composite store that which you want to belong to you.

*Fourth,* see your life as a unique expression. Seek to express your own talents, enlarge your own meaning, and discover your own values, without trying to do everything that everyone else is doing. You may be measuring up unfavorably with others because you are using their measuring rule. Don't try to walk in another's shoes, regardless of how desirable they may seem to be. Try to fill your own shoes more adequately.

*Fifth,* know that the subconscious can guide you to success when you direct it to do so. Program your mind with a guidance-request, affirming with Emerson that:

> Each man has his own vocation. The talent is the call. . . . He is like a ship in a river; he runs against obstructions on every side but one. On that side all obstruction is taken away and he sweeps serenely over a deepening channel into an infinite sea.[4]

Use the mind-processing card found earlier in this chapter to guide you to the channel that is free of obstacles and is awaiting your discovery.

*Sixth,* believe in a power greater than yourself. This is essential to a feeling of adequacy. However, you can believe in a power greater than you and still be fearful, isolated, and insecure, if you do not see your life as one with that power. To say that life is adequate and then leave yourself out of the picture, will not dissolve your insecurity. A conscious feeling of oneness must be established.

For example, a leaf may look at the trunk of the tree and affirm that it is greater than itself. This will give the leaf little satisfaction unless it also affirms that it is one with the tree. So it is with man. As a leaf on the tree of life, he will derive little security from the fact until he

I now awaken to the newness of this moment, strong in the knowledge that I need not acquiesce to mass influences around me. I declare my freedom from all preprogramming that others have done for me. I now reprogram my mind with new desires that embody the truth about me. I am a free, creative, inventive, unique, and radiant expression of life!

*Mental Data Processing Card No. 16*

asserts that he is one with the tree and has all of its life force to back him up.

*Seventh,* use Mental Data Processing Card No. 16 to focus your attention on what is true about yourself and to awake from preprogrammed data in the mass mind:

### Preprogrammed influences from others around you

Others are very fond of preprogamming your mind— of planning the thoughts that you should think. This pre-programming appears in the form of suggestions from friends, mental coercion from family, hints from the boss, propaganda, editorials, and advertising. Be it the soft sell or the hard sell, suggestion aimed at programming the subconscious is used. Think of the many brands of cosmetics, beverages, and drugs all purporting to be the best. Daily the public mind is processed with data which claims that "brand X is better than brand Y."

Influence is exerted by sales organizations, by political philosophies, by religious movements, and pressure groups—pulling first one way and then another. Their hope is to subconsciously motivate man in the direction they would like him to go. They seek to preprogram his mind for their own purposes.

This preprogramming is often subtle and indirect. The true motive behind it may not be apparent. It is slipped in undercover to manipulate public opinion without appearing to do so. Experiments in this subliminal type of motivation have demonstrated its effectiveness. For example, in one controlled experiment, the words "EAT MORE POPCORN" were flashed on a movie screen every few frames during the length of a film. On the nights this subliminal motivation was used, popocorn sales went up significantly.

Less subtle but quite effective is motivation based upon desire, association, and identification. The beautiful girl stretched out on the beach is so desirable that the product she is selling is desirable by association—buy "Puff 'n Koff," the new long-burning throat cigarette! The nattily dressed sea captain leaning against his magnificent yacht bespeaks such quality that surely the public will yearn to identify with that quality by buying the drink he is sipping, "Old Crumbling Barns" !

## How to dehypnotize your subconscious

In the process of awaking from your daytime sleep and dehypnotizing the subconscious, you will be amazed at the extent of your hypnosis. Advertising propaganda is one of the easier forms of suggestion to recognize. It is immediately apparent that the beauty pictured in the beach advertisement is posed there to sell cigarettes and not merely to delight the eye.

It may not be so apparent that suggestion from past associates still exerts influence and that hypnotic eyes make themselves felt from the environment. Man is literally swimming in a sea of mind, surrounded by ideas from the ages and heir to its mixed blessings. Emerson said, "Thoughts rule the world." [5] Whose thoughts rule you? They will be your own, if you assert your independence and reject the hypnotic spell of mass thinking. Too many people are walking around in a condition of trance induced by hypnotists who have long since passed on. Daily, people succumb to hypnotic signals within society, religion, economics, and politics.

And don't underestimate the power of subtle suggestion issuing from the press, radio, and television. Actual experiments with hypnosis have demonstrated that a hypnotist can practice his art without actual contact. Arthur J. Snider, reporting in *The Denver Post,* [6] tells of an experiment conducted between a subject and two psychiatrists who hypnotized their patient via television, demonstrating that an operator need not be present to put someone in a trance.

Although the deep hypnotic sleep induced by these two psychiatrists can not be equated with the milder suggestibility induced by mass thoughts, it is significant that suggestion can be transmitted without physical contact. Strong, dominant minds have influenced the thinking of suggestible minds throughout time.

It might be said that man's struggle is a struggle to free himself from the hypnotic spell of the past. This is not to say that the past is all negative. Certainly not! But man

165

should seek to dehypnotize his mind from a carry-over of limiting ideas that would inhibit his forward progress.

In mental cybernetics, you are not trying to convince yourself that you are better than those who have gone before. Indeed, you are standing now on the shoulders of many strong men and women. But, by virtue of their strength, you should be able to see farther than they were able to see. In any event, you are better than you know. You are stronger than you realize. You possess powers of which you have never dreamed—perhaps simply because you have never dreamed big enough.

## CHAPTER SUMMARY OF POINTS TO PONDER

1. At an early age man falls victim to hypnotic "eyes"—not only to the conscious views of others such as parents, teachers, and counselors, but to things such as environmental factors and the atmosphere of feeling around him.

2. Hypnotic suggestions may come from man's own conscious mind, since it is the initiator of action, or from the mind of another who possesses undue influence over him.

3. Post-hypnotic impressions have been programmed into man's mind by people he has never seen and by experiences he submitted to unconsciously.

4. Since the nature of the subconscious mind is to act upon premises programmed into it, regardless of their source, ideas from the minds of others to which man has acquiesced may be the cause of his unhappiness, limitation, or failure.

5. Man's goal is to awaken from his daytime sleep, from the hypnotic spell cast by the world of experience and condition, and become aware of his full potentialities.

6. To break the hold of habit thought that binds him to a monotonous repetition of experience, man should ask, "Who's using my mind?" Then he should assert his independence from any influence that would limit him.

7. The power of negative thought which in primitive societies has been called the hex, voodoo, or the evil eye, is real only to the extent that man gives it reality by believing it.

8. Man can become his own hypnotist by claiming full conscious control over his subconscious mind and by commanding it to screen out negative data that he may encounter.

9. Man need not succumb to the complexes of desire and memory that would distort his personality—poverty complex, persecution complex, accident-prone complex, inferiority complex, and the like. To free himself from the mistaken data that mass thought would tell him about himself, he must awaken to the truth of his being. Man is not inferior to another. He is not superior to another. He is free to make inferior use of his mind, and he is free to make superior use of his potentialities.

10. Man should think of himself not as being better than another or of being less than another. He should think of himself as being different from all others! Each man is a special, unique, and distinct pattern of individualized life, possessing potentialities of unlimited expression.

# CHAPTER NINE

## *How to De-Automate
Your False Attitudes*

Robert Louis Stevenson was physically frail all his life. As a child, he was kept indoors much of the time. He spent his days reading or sitting quietly and often dreamed of what he wanted to do when he became a man. In the evening, his favorite pasttime was watching the lamplighter at work kindling the lamps along the street. Young Robert pressed his face against the windowpane, following the man as he lit each lamp one by one.

One night, noticing the boy's rapt attention as he gazed out the window, the nurse asked him what he was doing. The youthful Stevenson replied, "I'm watching the man knock holes in the darkness."

Today, central switches are thrown at dusk and cities are instantly ablaze with street lights. Things are different, ways have changed, progress and mechanization are in full sway. Strange, isn't it, that the lamplighter, as Stevenson thought of him, is still needed. There is a need for anyone who can bring light to the dark places of ignorance, suspicion, antagonism, and prejudice. The world is desperate for lamplighters who can knock holes in the darkness of man's discontent.

**Dissolving the darkness of discontent**

There is a darkness of discontent abroad in our world that needs a lot of holes knocked in it. Better than mere holes, of course, would be the complete illumination of every dark corner in man's mental realm. Discontent today is a disease, and almost everyone is infected with it to some degree.

Some of this discontent may be due to the vast and rapid changes that have taken place in the life of mankind of a scientific, philosophical, and technological nature. Generically, man has been uprooted from a simpler, less pressured life and thrust into the complications of a fast-paced, competitive environment. Bewilderment, frustration, hostility, and discontent have resulted. In his bewilderment, man runs hither and yon looking for an answer to his problems. Ironically, he is not quite sure what his problems are. Frequently he feels that if he can manipulate the external world, he can bring his problems to an end. So he espouses this cause and that cause. He turns to this "'ism" or that "ism," to this panacea and that panacea, while darkness turns to midnight.

## The use of new-attitude therapy

How can this discontent be dispelled? How can this darkness be sublimated into light? "With," I would unhesitatingly declare, "a change of attitude." All of the major problems of today would be either partly or totally solved by a change of attitude. The changing of the world (en masse) awaits the changing of man (the individual). The world will become better when better individuals come forth to brighten it. The world is a cinemascope production of the individual life—expanded and multiplied by the number in the cast. The wide-angle lense catches every corner—the bright and the shadowy—and produces the montage called mankind.

The interrelatedness of mankind is self-evident. However, for each person, life remains an individual proposition and his unique philosophy is a personal matter. This means that each person must look within himself to find the cause which, in union with others who have found the cause within, will create better effects in the world. This cause lies in the area of attitude—a change of attitude for you.

There is one attitude, one paramount outlook, that will

169

make all your other attitudes sane, practical, and productive of good. This is the attitude of life taught by mental cybernetics. It is the heartfelt outlook that universal mind power responds to your use of it. Universal mind responds reciprocally to individual awareness, to your self-image, and to your desire-demands. Mind power acts creatively upon your desires and reflects them back to you in terms of experience. The Psalmist understood this reflective activity of universal creativeness to individual thought when he said, "With the loyal thou dost show thyself loyal; with the blameless man thou dost show thyself blameless; with the pure thou dost show thyself pure; and with the crooked thou dost show thyself perverse." [1]

In the parable of the Prodigal Son, this reciprocal, reflective action is symbolized as the response of a father to a son. After the son's decision to arise from his misery and return unto the father, the father's response is couched in this poetic thought, "The Father, seeing him afar off, ran to meet him." [2] This is more than poetry, however. It is symbolic of the eager response of universal mind to the individual's choices and decisions. There is a correspondence, there is a reciprocal activity, there is a rushing to meet the individual on the part of universal creativeness when the individual corrects his beliefs, attitudes, desires, and awareness.

The Psalmist and the Speaker of Parables both present a poignant picture of the responsiveness of life toward the attitudes with which the individual programs his mind. The son in the parable changed his misery to happiness with a change of attitude. By using this same therapy— by correcting old outlooks with new attitudes—you can change your life.

### Your magic mirror of mind

If you wish to undertake new-attitude therapy, you must first understand how much your attitudes really matter. You must realize how life reflects back to you the outlooks you hold.

Imagine that the room where you are now sitting is lined with mirrors. The ceiling is a mirror, and when you look up you see yourself. The floor is a mirror, and when you look down you see yourself. The walls are lined with mirrors, and when you look to the right or left, you see your own reflection. When you look ahead of you, you see your image, and when you turn around, you see yourself. In other words, the world you see as experience is a reflection of the individual who sees it, together with many of the viewpoints man holds collectively. You see not so much with your physical sight, but with your attitudes of mind.

It might be said that the only world that exists for you is that which you are able to see with the mind's eye. And the place where you stand as you view the world is at that spot where your attitudes "place" you.

## Your attitudes can be alleys or allies

The attitudes you hold toward life are the most important creative factors in your personal world. By your attitudes, you are either walking down the alleys and backroads of life, experiencing limitation, unhappiness, and frustration, or, through the cultivation of mountain-top attitudes, you are traveling the highway of success. By your attitudes, you determine the major programs you feed into the computer of creative mind. Negative attitude-programming may cause your life to move along the side streets of resentment, self-pity, and failure, where you are denied those values that make life rich and meaningful. On the other hand, positive attitudes—attitudes that affirm life—become allies that invite the riches of the universe into your personal experience.

| *Affirmative Attitudes* | *Adverse Attitudes* |
|---|---|
| A-ppreciation | A-ntagonism |
| T-houghtfulness | T-houghtlessness |
| T-ranquility | T-ension |
| I-dentification | I-mpatience |
| T-hankfulness | T-hanklessness |
| U-nification | U-ncooperativeness |
| D-ecisiveness | D-iscouragement |
| E-mpathy | E-nvy |
| S-elf-esteem | S-elf-depreciation |

Pause now to analyze your attitudes. Use the two contrasting attitude lists below and give a few moments' thought to each outlook. Do you tend to identify more with the affirmative list, with those attitudes that assure a life of peace, poise, and power? Or do you tend to identify with items in the negative list, with those adverse attitudes that poison the personality and deny the individual the good that life can bring?

## Appreciation attitudes

Where can you begin to knock holes in the darkness of your mental world? Is there any better point of beginning than with the cultivation of appreciation? To appreciate means "to set a just value on; to esteem to the full worth of." [3] Have you set a just value on yourself? Do you esteem the full worth of the gift of life that belongs to you?

You are the user of a power that you did not create. You are the beneficiary of values that were here when you arrived. You are the recipient of multiple gifts—from the richness of the soil that grows your food, the oil that flows from the depths of the earth, and the wealth that is extracted from the seas, to the wondrous body that serves you with five spectacular faculties. You are on the receiving end of life! And there is no limitation to those gifts intended for you. The potential is endless! The only limitation is the limitation of your own ability to receive and the ability you experience in association with others around you.

Life can do for you only what it can do through you, and your appreciation-attitude increases your ability to receive. To appreciate the good that belongs to you— to place a just value on your work, on your talents, on your freedom, on those who love you, and on those who share in living this life with you—is to set in motion a law of mind that enhances every facet of life for you.

What may the adverse attitude of antagonism produce in your life? Can it, by its very nature, produce anything other than hostility? Possibly you can recall someone who is antagonistic toward life. He lives with a chip on his shoulder, the world owes him a living, his wants are ignored, life is unfair, and the universe is all wrong. The universe, of course, has not set itself in opposition to such a person. It is his attitude that makes of life a hostile enemy or a friend. The universe responds by a correspondence, a co-response. His antagonism creates its own wall, and it places on that wall the enemy that must oppose him.

Appreciation can be used to knock holes in the wall of antagonism wherever it may appear. Appreciation dissolves darkness as the sun disperses fog. Cultivate an affirmative attitude toward life, toward other members of your family, toward your work, and your ability to do and to be, and you will find fewer and fewer antagonistic experiences around you.

## Thoughtfulness attitudes

From a practical viewpoint, to be thoughtful is to be full of thought—to give the mind over to thinking. "Thought means life," wrote A. B. Alcott, "since those who do not think do not live in any high or real sense. Thinking makes the man." [4] The Thinking person considers others; the thoughtless person seldom properly considers himself. To be thoughtful is to affirm the rights and freedom of others. It is also to give proper consideration to your own rights as they fit into a scheme of cooperation and harmony.

The thoughtless person negates friendship. He takes from others without giving, and eventually there is no one remaining from whom to take. Although he wants the attention of others, his attitude of thoughtlessness denies him the concern that he would like others to feel for him.

### CASE HISTORY OF A THOUGHTLESS PERSON

Ellen was a typically thoughtless person. It is strange that she did not recognize it, for she herself had been thoughtlessly rejected as a child. Ellen's father left her mother when Ellen was ten years of age. Her mother got a divorce and remarried two years later. Half-brothers and sisters came along to occupy the center of the scene. The stage seemed too small to accommodate Ellen.

Searching for someone who would love her, Ellen married young. Within two years she was back home—a home where she was appreciated even less than before. She married again, determined to secure from life what she felt was coming to her. But this attempt also ended in failure.

It was Ellen's attitude toward life that worked against her. She was not considerate of the rights and freedom of others. As a daughter, she resented the things done for her half-brothers and sisters. As a wife, she was possessive and insisted on the exclusive attention of her husband. She demanded her full rights but cared little about the rights of others. She lacked a thoughtful approach to life and toward other people, and hence few other people responded with thoughtfulness toward her. Remember, life corresponds, reflects, and responds to one's attitudes. Life is like that room full of mirrors that reflect from every angle.

Ellen's world reflected the dark, shadowy corners of thoughtlessness that she practiced. Her attitude might have been called selfishness, yet it did not really serve her self-interest. With her outlook she cut off friendship, love, appreciation, and companionship. In her selfishness, she wasn't even serving the self intelligently, for she ended up unhappy and alone. A change of attitude would have knocked holes in that darkness and brought her the love and responsiveness for which she longed.

## How to tranquilize your troubles

The practice of tranquillity is desperately needed in the world today. It is the only tranquilizer that can knock permanent holes in the darkness of tension and pressure. A sense of well-being that brings happiness as a by-product depends upon the stability of the emotional center. Man is governed more by the way he feels than by the way he thinks. His thinking is often subservient to his emotions. The feeling center and the thinking center act and react upon each other.

To break the hold of the emotional center, the conscious-thinking center must assume command. New attitudes must be programmed into the subconscious to replace the commands implanted by emotional reactions. Remember, the normal condition of the subconscious is a hypnotized state—that is, the subconscious is obedient and responsive to suggestion. Hence, you want to be sure that the subconscious is receiving the type of suggestions you wish it to follow and not indiscriminate, negative drives from the emotional center. This was Ellen's mistake.

## STEPS FOR TRANQUILLITY THERAPY

To begin self-treatment with the therapy of tranquillity:

*First,* declare that you are in conscious command of your life. Look into a mirror, and, if there is a frown of tension on your brow, wipe it off. If there is a stoop of defeat or an air of burden about you, square your shoulders and take a stance which makes you feel that you are the boss. Put a smile on your face and assume a new physical posture of peace and poise. Soon your new physical posture will be reflected as a new inner feeling of power.

*Second,* consider the source of most tension. Tension is defined as a "state or degree of being strained to stiffness." [5] Tension often is due to an attempt to carry too great a load, straining not only with current burdens but also with a load of troubles from the past. Tranquillity is achieved through a daily clearing of past accounts. For example: Let's say that after shopping at a supermarket, you wheeled your cart of groceries to the check stand. If the checker started to ring up your account without first clearing the previous purchase, you would quickly tell him of his error. Yet how often a previous experience is not cleared.

The angry husband who has an argument with his wife at breakfast may carry over the account to the office where tensions develop because of his emotional state. The driver provoked by the car in front of him may carry forward the account, and consequently may growl

175

and grumble about the traffic the whole way to work. The attainment of tranquillity requires the diligent clearing of the subconscious register after each encounter with life. Don't carry over from one experience to another the tensions and burdens of the previous encounter. Today is a fresh moment in time. Greet it with a consciousness cleared of past mistakes, a consciousness uncluttered, unburdened, and unprogrammed by negative carry-over.

*Third,* to gain tranquillity, practice release. A very wise man centuries ago said, "There is a time for everything under the sun." [6] There is a time to deal with your problem, and there is a time to forget about it. Don't let a business problem intrude into every moment of your personal time. Don't take a problem to bed with you. Release it in its time. There are people who seem to feel that their problem is eternal. When a situation arises that must be dealt with, handle it and then release it. It is true, indeed, that worry is the interest paid by those who borrow trouble.

*Fourth,* tranquillity therapy requires the practice of relaxation. A relaxed attitude is essential to happiness, to health, and a sense of well-being. Physical relaxation may be attained through recreation, exercise, and contemplation of beauty, art, and music. Mental relaxation may be gained through meditation and quiet realization of the grandeur of life. The goal of relaxation, please note, is not a passivity of mind, but a resetting of the

I now breathe deeply and relax, one by one, the muscles throughout the length of my body. As I inhale anew, I gain a feeling of peace and poise. As I exhale, I release all tensions and pressure. I close my eyes and a wondrous sense of tranquillity enfolds me. Darkness disappears and my mind is flooded with well-being.

*Mental Data Processing Card No. 17*

176

mind. Relaxation should bring a redirecting of the mind through inner attention. Learn to pause and pay some inner attention to your moods, attitudes and feelings. All too often, man is so preoccupied with outward conditions and situations that his inner moods and attitudes slip by unmonitored. Pause and challenge those moods and feelings that are negative and tension-producing, and reject them! Then, reset the mind; redirect it toward poise and peace.

Use Mental Data Processing Card No. 17 to tranquilize your mind, to relax, to release problems, and to knock holes in the darkness of tension and pressure.

### How to build a bigger identity for yourself

On what is your identity built? In the process of mental programming do you say "I" to states of mind or qualities of being that are uncomplimentary? Are there times when you affirm, "I am impatient; I am short-tempered; I am irritated; I am disgusted"? The individual who again and again identifies himself with undesirable states of being may soon find it difficult to separate himself from those identified states.

Begin now to practice the therapy of new attitudes toward yourself by building a bigger identity. Base your identity not upon a small, assumed self that has been constructed of false self-images affirmed over the years. Rather, base your evaluation of yourself upon the highest potentials within you.

An identification that acknowledges your real self gives you a sense of poise, patience, and command. You are a place where the universal mind principle has come forth as an individual. Thus your potentials are unlimited. They reach back to the universal, and you latently have all the power, all the resources, all the ideas, and all the time you will ever need to make your dreams come true. To realize this gives you a feeling of command that dissolves all impatience, irritation, and ill temper. To identify with this gives you a feeling of bigness toward others and toward life that leaves no room for petty irritability.

If you tend to feel impatient with others and frustrated in self-fulfillment, here are three things to do to de-automate your irritations:

*First,* realize that you are not what you have identified yourself as being in the past. You are the identifier, not the identified. You are the observer, not the observed. You are the programmer, not the program. The real self, in the final analysis, is in command and can change the program.

*Second,* realize that while you have identified yourself as being a certain type of person—perhaps even to the point of becoming type-cast—you are still free to choose the role that you want to play in life. Your potentials transcend all previous identifications.

*Third,* your life is an inseparable part of a universal process. Identify yourself with this greater principle. Let that principle operate for you by consciously affirming your oneness with those constructive states of being that you want to make your own. Only with greater ideas can you build a bigger identity.

## Thankfulness-thinking attitudes

Another effective way to knock holes in the darkness of mental night is to practice the attitude of gratitude. The man who prospers is the one who brings to each day a consciousness of praise and thanksgiving. He is the one who knows that the horn of plenty is filled with an unlimited potential and he is its heir.

The writer of Proverbs said, "He who tends a fig tree will eat its fruit, and a man is judged by his praise." [7] As a man tending a fig tree will eat its fruit, so will man mentally partake of the values he tends. What he looks at mentally and remembers becomes the quality of thinking that bears fruit.

Consider the word *praise.* To praise means to extol, to laud, to magnify, and to eulogize. Your life prospers in those things, those conditions and experiences, which you extol, magnify, and dwell upon. This does not apply only to good qualities, but to all qualities.

What do you extol? What do you remember, eulogize, and magnify? Memory is wonderful, if you remember rightly. But, if you remember only wrongs and hurts, the law of the subconscious mind must perpetuate the wrongs remembered. The present is the result of the way you have remembered the past. It is not so much the past itself, but the way you interpret the past that bears upon the present. A person with a negative consciousness will interpret events, conditions, and experiences negatively; whereas the person with an affirmative attitude toward life will interpret these same events and experiences positively.

Therefore, to de-automate thanklessness and cultivate the attitude of gratitude, look for things in the past for which you can give thanks. In this act is found the seed of an abundant harvest. If you want health, happiness, love, understanding, abundance of supply, peaceful surroundings, and happy relationships, you must tend them to eat their fruit. Plant the seed of gratitude for every blessing you can now identify. Tend it with praise, and watch it grow.

Be on the lookout for thankfulness. It can postpone and even cancel the good for which you long. The person who remarks, "I have precious little to be thankful for," is planting a negative thought command. The lonely woman who longs for love and companionship but laments, "I can't be happy until I find a good husband," is postponing her happiness, for what man wants an unhappy wife? The man who declares, "This is a thankless job," is cancelling out his raise with the attitude that his boss does not appreciate him. Practice a feeling of happiness and gratitude, and happiness will come looking for you.

### How to unify with what you desire

To achieve the good you want from life, you must become one with that good. You must unify or coalesce with your desire. You must become one with the quality of life that you would make your own.

You have learned that in using the science of mental cybernetics, you must program your mind with the self-image you wish. However, until you really believe in that self-image and sincerely unify with it, it will remain a wishy-washy idea that brings no results. Change your wishes into reality by unifying with them and acting *as if*. Plan *as if* you expected your desire to be demonstrated. Behave *as if* your desire is already accomplished. Cooperate with your mental program by preparing yourself. If you need training, get it. If you need additional education, enroll for it. In every way, cooperate by acting as if your desire is a reality.

It is a basic law of mental cybernetics that *to have more you must become more*. Your self-image determines its own result. Therefore, to have more you must unify with a greater self-image. Think and your thoughts become things; be and your being takes form as experience.

In a previous chapter, you began working on a desire-demand list, listing those things you want from life and impressing those demands upon the creative level of the subconscious. In the process of demonstrating, you must unify with your desires until they become a part of you and you become one with them. Your desiring must change to unification. For to be forever desiring without *being* what you desire, will lead only to frustration.

For example, if your desire calls for more money, what must you *be* in order to demonstrate more? You might list any number of *being* qualities essential to your having money, such as *being* more knowledgeable, more skillful, more commanding, more personable, etc. These qualities you must embody if you are to have the more you desire. To embody is to coalesce with the desire you seek to demonstrate, and to coalesce is "to grow together into one body." [8] To have the thing, you must be it—you must equal it in mind.

In working with your desire-demand list, watch out for uncooperativeness. You are uncooperative with your heart's desire if you fail to do the muscular. For example, a widow wished to sell her large home. She listed it with realtor after realtor, yet an entire year passed with no buyer. Finally, she realized that she was not cooperating with her desire. She had made no effort to clean the attic and clear the basement of the accumu-

180

lation of a half-century of living. She began to act *as if*—as if she was really going to sell. She did the muscular; she unified with her desire by starting to sort out and pack. Within two weeks, a buyer appeared and the house was sold.

Uncooperativeness shows up in many ways. It manifests sometimes as a feeling of separation and withdrawal. The employee who wishes to work his way up in the company and yet does not feel that he is a unified part of the business will find his desires thwarted. He is the person who says, "*They* aren't running it right! *They* don't manage this well! *They* have the wrong policy about that!" He separates himself from the business. He stands on one side, and *they* stand on the other. To succeed and rise to the top, an employee should unify in thought and action with the company he serves. He should cultivate a "we" attitude. He should be able to say, "This is the way *we* do business. These are the policies *we* have." If he wishes to be included in the management of the business, he must include himself in the interests of the company.

### How to make decisive attitudes work for your success

Robert Gair, shortly after immigrating to this country from Scotland, began adding value to our national wealth by revolutionizing the packaging industry. He made the first folding paper box, and its use spread quickly. Buying a cheap printing press, he next started the practice of putting merchants' names on paper bags. Needless to say, he became a millionaire. In large bold type, the letters P.I.T.T.O.T. adorned his office. This was Robert Gair's motto. When he had a decision to make, he would look at these letters. What did they mean? "Procrastination is the thief of time."

Procrastination is more than the thief of time. It steals happiness, it destroys initiative, and it breeds discouragement. Indecision can be a major cause of failure in all departments of life. Indecision can become a negative habit. A person can spend endless time going around and around with the question, "What shall I do?" Some people seem to be forever on the fence, even with mere trifles.

*First,* to de-automate indecision and cultivate decisiveness, remember that the power of decision is an inherent right. Life gives unto each person the right of choice. This right is yours as an individualization of universal mind. Claim it and exercise it joyously.

*Second,* this right and responsibility is present and constant. You cannot make a decision today that will take care of the next ten years. Each day will demand certain decisions of you.

*Third,* in making decisions, become aware that you do not stand alone. Therefore, you are not deficient in wisdom or lacking in power. The whole principle of universal mind stands back of you, plus the accumulated wisdom of mankind, and, in addition, the knowledge of your own personalized experience.

*Fourth,* take time to consider the things you have to do. Meditate upon them. Draw upon the wisdom that is yours, and then decide. Whatever the decision may be—whether it is changing jobs, moving to another part of the country, selecting a life partner—know that a deeper wisdom motivates your action. To tap that wisdom, program a guidance request into the subconscious. Let it lead you along the path of right fulfillment, and you may be sure that your decision will not be false.

*Fifth,* secure in mind the end result of what you want to achieve, and the guidance principle of the subconscious will fill out the in-between steps for its accomplishment. If the goal is secured in mind, the way to that goal is assured!

### Empathy vs envy attitudes

Empathy is the ability to understand how another feels, without feeling as the other feels. It is more than sympathy, for sympathy may cause a man to enter into the problem of another. It is not climbing down into the ditch with the one who has a problem but standing on the bank and extending a helping hand. The empathic attitude is one of understanding for the less fortunate and one of rejoicing for those who have achieved.

182

Its opposite, envy, is one of the most deadly of the false attitudes that man must conquer. It is a denial of the good life. In effect, the envious person is saying, "I am jealous of you and the good you have in life *because you have it instead of me.*" He thinks of the universe as a rationing system, and since the good he wants has already been rationed out to another, he feels cheated.

Because the envious person is saying, "I cannot have because you have," he will not have. For, mentally, he desires to deny another. The jealous person is not aware that his desire to deny another reacts as denial upon himself. One law applies for all—yourself and others. You cannot hold another person down without staying down with him to some extent.

Condemnation often accompanies envy. The jealous individual tends to condemn his neighbor who is enjoying happiness and success. In his twisted thinking, he may begin to feel that something is wrong with wealth because he does not have it. He may even come to believe that happiness is wicked and riches are sinful. When this happens, his condemnation works against his chances of success for he finds himself wanting the things he feels it is wrong to have. Thus he denies himself the very good he desires.

To have empathy is to affirm others in their achievements. To rejoice in the good of another is to open your life to a like good. What you affirm for another, you affirm for yourself. What you deny another, you deny yourself.

### The success attitude of self-esteem

A Russian writer tells of a brilliant musician who, in performing for a group of friends, played with such feeling that a sense of reverence pervaded the room. After he stopped, there was silence—a silence broken finally by the musician himself as he attempted to entertain his listeners with a ribald story. One of his companions, reflecting the attitude of the others, said: "Be quiet, please! You are not worthy to be yourself."

You are worthy to be yourself, even when isolated incidents seem to prove otherwise. But you must look beyond the self that you ordinarily see to find the esteem-worthy real self. Self-esteem is not a matter of basking in your own glory but a matter of beholding the vastness of your life as it can be. No individual can expand his own evaluation of himself unless he has an expanded source to which he looks for his expanded evaluation.

The universe has given rise to the individualized expression of life that you are. However, this individualization mirrors only minutely the inherent possibilities of its source. As a drop of water is the same as the ocean in essence, so your life in essence is one with the potentialities of universal mind. Evolution's labors, through millions of years, have culminated in the individual production of you.

Recognize that your life is important. It has meaning. That you have not discovered its meaning does not prove its meaning is nonexistent. It only proves that you have not made an important discovery.

The person who has not discovered the wonder and worth of his own unique individualization is an easy prey to self-depreciation. He belittles and condemns himself. He is hesitant and short on confidence. He is aware only of the assumed, superficial self built through his contact with society and environment and knows nothing of the real self and its latent values.

The ancients recognized the importance of self-esteem and admonished, "Man, know thyself." In chapter two of this book, you were directed to write a description of yourself that you might "know thyself" better. To know yourself better is to identify the false so it can be discarded and to identify the real so it can be cultivated. In cultivating the real self, a sense of esteem must be developed—an esteem built upon a vision of the greatness to which the real self may rise.

To esteem means to "appreciate the worth of; to hold in high regard." [9] Self-esteem cannot be built upon the shifting sands of ego reactions. It is built on that which undergirds the ego—the real self, the larger self that knows its greatness. Any man can say, "I can." But the one who knows the I which says, "I can," is the one who will never know failure, defeat, insecurity, self-depreciation, and inadequacy. It is this larger self that you are

184

required to appreciate and hold in high regard if you are to de-automate the false attitude of self-depreciation.

### Your attitude altimeter reading

On the Attitude Altimeter (an indicator of heights and depths) that follows, you will find listed along the top nine affirmative attitudes just discussed and, along the bottom, nine negative counterparts. Did you, as each attitude was mentioned, tend to recognize positive and adverse attitudes that you may hold?

Review now the nine affirmative values on the Attitude Altimeter below. As you consider them one by one, put an X in the light square to indicate any of those outlooks you honestly can claim as attitudes you generally hold. That is, if you usually show appreciation for the efforts of others, put an X in that square. Do the same for the others—thoughtfulness, tranquillity, identification, thankfulness, unification, decisiveness, empathy, and self-esteem.

Next, consider the adverse values on the lower side of the Attitude Altimeter. They are indicated by dark squares and represent the darkness lurking in the mental night of mind. Consider the nine bottom attitudes one by one, and, being honest with yourself, put an X in the shaded square that indicates a negative quality you may harbor.

Then compare the upper light scale to the lower dark scale. Do you need more X's on the light side? Do you need to knock more holes in the darkness of your attitudes? At what points do you need to replace negative

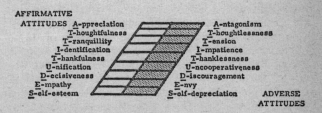

AFFIRMATIVE
ATTITUDES   A-ppreciation                    A-ntagonism
            T-houghtfulness                  T-houghtlessness
            T-ranquillity                    T-ension
            I-dentification                  I-mpatience
            T-hankfulness                    T-hanklessness
            U-nification                     U-ncooperativeness
            D-ecisiveness                    D-iscouragement
            E-mpathy                         E-nvy
            S-elf-esteem                     S-elf-depreciation   ADVERSE
                                                                 ATTITUDES

*Attitude Altimeter*

No. 18.

outlooks with positive ones? Rate your attitudes by means of the Attitude Altimeter, and then correct adverse attitudes by using Mental Data Processing Card

I now identify with a self that is too big to harbor unworthy attitudes. It is a self too fine to be petty—too thoughtful to be ungracious. I knock holes in the darkness of discontent around me by programming my mind with complimentary attitudes and rejecting the automated grip of negative outlooks.

*Mental Data Processing Card No. 18*

## CHAPTER SUMMARY OF POINTS TO PONDER

1. Negative emotions, ignorance, and discontent cast their darkness abroad. Man, with positive emotions and understanding, can knock holes in this darkness and clear it away.

2. Each man must become his own lamplighter, sublimating the dark areas of his life into desirable experiences through the practice of new-attitude therapy. A change of attitude can change man's life!

3. To practice new-attitude therapy, man must examine the daily attitudes he holds, recognize them for what they are—affirmative or adverse—and honestly discard the ones that are detrimental.

4. Antagonism must be discarded and replaced with the practice of appreciation. To appreciate is to set a just value on or to esteem the full worth of a thing—of oneself, of friends, of blessings, and of life itself.

5. Thoughtlessness must be discarded and replaced with thoughtfulness. The thoughtful man affirms

186

the rights and freedom of others and gives proper consideration to his own rights as they fit into a scheme of harmony for all.

6. Tension must give way to tranquillity. A tranquil attitude toward life can be gained by clearing from the register of mind past accounts of tension, strain, and worry before ringing up a new sale.

7. A self-identity that is too big for impatience and pettiness must be sought. When man identifies with something greater than himself, the little irritations and frustrations of life disappear.

8. Thanklessness must be discarded and replaced with thankfulness. Gratitude and thanksgiving tend to magnify the good for which thanks is given. In the attitude of gratitude is found the seed of an abundant harvest.

9. Uncooperativeness with the law of good must give way to unification with it. To achieve the good he wants from life, man must become one with that good—he must unify with it. To have more, he must be more.

10. Discouragement and indecision must be discarded and replaced with decisiveness. Life gives to each man the right of choice. It is his responsibility to use the power of decision and to use it wisely.

11. Envy attitude must give way to empathy. To envy is to covet the good of another; to have empathy is to affirm others in their achievement of good.

12. Self-depreciation must be discarded and replaced with self-esteem. To esteem the self is not to bask in the glory of present achievements, but to behold the vastness of the real self as it can be.

# CHAPTER TEN

*How Mental Cybernetics
Can Make Your Will-
power Work For You*

At some time in your life, you are bound to meet a
person like George. George was a dreamer of big dreams.
He was the possessor of an active imagination, and ideas,
plans, schemes, and propositions gushed forth from his
mind in an unending stream.

Like the eruption of Old Faithful at Yellowstone National Park, George was regular. One glorious idea would
barely be undertaken when it was abandoned for another
far more glamorous. And, if you needed an idea, George
had it. If you mentioned a tentative plan for making
money, George's active imagination was right in there
planning for you.

With each job—and George was in and out of more
jobs than anyone I know—he was always going to make
a million. The selling field was his forte. He sold insur-
ance; he sold books; he sold household appliances.
Whatever there was to be sold, at some time George
had sold it.

With each new venture, this was to be the big one.
This time he'd reach success! In his imagination, he'd
plan what he would do with all of the money he was
going to make. He'd talk in such flowing terms that his
wife would once again take heart and believe that things
were moving toward success for them.

But with each new scheme, his dreams fell through
as they had previously. Finally his wife, tired of trying to
live on dreams, divorced dreamy George and married

Solid Sam, who was working for a salary. The salary was small compared to George's grandiose plans, but the weekly check was regular and provided a comfortable life.

## How to make the will discipline imagination

Was George wrong in his dreaming? The answer must be no. Where would mankind be without its dreamers? Without its men of imagination and vision? Imagination has enabled man to move upward to the position he occupies today. The land, the sea, the sky are filled with the products of man's imagination. Imagination is the creative faculty of the mind. But something more than imagination is needed if practical results are to be achieved.

That something more which is needed is the *will* to discipline the imaginative faculty. Without discipline, the imagination is like a plane without a pilot. It may fly, but where will it land? George could fly beautifully, but he crashed with each landing. His imagination was undisciplined. He could soar, but no one stayed at the controls to guide the flight unerringly to its destination. George had not learned to combine perseverance with his imaginative faculty. He took off in flights of fancy that were not stable enough to persist until he reached his goal. He was not in control of his imagination. His imagination controlled him.

## What keeps a good man down?

You have heard the expression, "You can't keep a good man down." This is not entirely true. There are many men and women with creative ideas who have not made the grade in life. One reason for this failure is the absence of disciplined imagination. Will power is the missing ingredient—the will to persevere in a dream until it becomes a reality.

Will power and perseverance, of course, are not to be mistaken for ruthlessness. Constructive use of will power will give you push without making you one of the "pushers" of the world. As a lad on the farm, I often heard the phrase, "The squeaking wheel gets the grease."

189

Many, believing this old adage, go through life squeaking. They make a loud noise; they elbow their way up the counter; they demand the attention of the clerk; they push their way to the front of the line. Pushers are those who fight their way to the top, oblivious of the many toes they step on, all for their pound of grease.

Of course, just as undesirable are the "Casper Milquetoasts"; you should never allow yourself to be used as a doormat or a bookmark. The constructive use of will power prevents you from being either spineless or obnoxiously pushy in exercising your freedom and achieving the success you desire.

However, it is essential that you learn how to make your will power work for you instead of against you. A person may have splendid ideas, he may have talent, he may have many things going for him, but if he has a weak and vacillating will, he may end up low man on the totem pole. A "good man" may find himself "kept down" if he lacks the will to persist in the dream his imagination has conceived.

### Mental photography and your will

In Chapter 2 of this book, you learned that the conscious mind uses the camera of imagination to photograph life. Your impressions of the world around you are filmed moment by moment as you go through the day. These impressions are caught by your imagination and colored by your attitudes, moods, prejudices, inclinations, and ambitions. These pictures are then developed in the darkroom of the subconscious and become your self-image. This self-image is the core concept around which the elements forming your personality gather to create the conditions and experiences of life.

Your self-conception is the most important fact in your life. To change your self-definition is to change your world of experience. As explained in Chapter 4, your inner life is like a house with many rooms. Lining the walls of those rooms are pictures—tracings of past experiences, self-portraits you have made, and drawings you have bought of other people's impressions of you.

The history of mankind, as well as your own personal

190

diary of experience, is stored in the picture room of your subconscious mind. From the inner images stored there by you, by the group of which you are a part, and by mass thinking from the nation and the world, outer events and experiences are projected. Your subconscious is a library of films, and life is the screen upon which your self-image is projected.

Thus, right mental photography—with the camera of constructive imagination—is essential to achieving any real success in life. But, once having filmed a clear picture of what you want to be or want to do, the dynamic of will must be employed to carry this picture into action. You must envision yourself as you want to be. Then you must persist in that vision with the use of disciplined will power.

## Your mental team of imagination and will power

Imagination and will power must be seen as an inseparable team; each is ineffective without the other. Imagination, without direction of will, builds castles without foundations. And will power, without imagination, works upon restricted material and achieves only limited success. The individual who has not developed imagination works at the direction of the imaginative faculty of other minds —producing the visions of others and fulfilling the dreams of other men. The individual who has not developed will power may have his own imaginative dreams, but, like George, he may not be able to carry those dreams to completion.

Imagination and will power, combined, work as a team like the fuel and steering wheel of the car you drive. The fuel that propels the vehicle is like your imagination, while the steering wheel is like your will. Without fuel in your car, you could not move down the highway, and, without the steering wheel, you could not hold the car to its destination. Similarly, without the fuel of imagination, you cannot move forward in life, and, without the steering wheel of will, you cannot hold yourself to your goal.

Your will power can hold you to the road, but it does not provide the magic spark that ignites you. Your

191

imagination provides that creative spark, but, alone, it very soon exhausts itself without the will to persist.

## What the will of universal mind is for you

What is the "will" of universal mind for you? Do you believe that the universe wills conditions for you that are in opposition to your good? Do you believe that the universe has placed restrictions upon you in regard to personality development and self-mastery? No such thing has happened. The universe is unlimited and holds infinite possibilities for you. The only restrictions that exist are those found in your own self-image and in the image mass consciousness may have impressed upon you.

You are the offspring of the one creative, infinite cause. As Emerson has said, "Of the universal mind each individual man is one more incarnation." [1] The universal impulsion of givingness has pressed itself forth as your awareness. Your life has become a door through which the givingness of life continues to flow.

However, the flow of life through you depends upon what you believe the universal "will" for you really is. You need accept nothing less than the limitless potential that the universe offers you. Through the right programming of mind, you can free yourself from the restriction that mass consciousness has falsely endorsed. You can choose to accept the full heritage of good that the universe holds for you. If you do, what is that heritage? What is your request from the universe?

That heritage is like a bequest from a beneficent father. Think of the universal mind from which you have sprung as the cause of you. It is the parent cause, the universal father. What is the father's will for you? This is how it might read:

> I, Universal Mind, as the Father of all life, being of sound mind, of infinite love and givingness, of supreme power, and of unlimited wisdom, do hereby grant to my son/daughter and heir all real and personal property belonging to my unlimited estate.

192

*This estate is free of all encumbrances, all taxes, and all obligations, other than these requirements as set forth below: Namely, that this estate shall be used for the increase of happiness, health, love, and understanding between the members of my family.*

*However, if my son/daughter, in his/her freedom, should mortgage this inheritance through negative attitudes, false ideas and limiting concepts in any of the many areas of its unlimited wealth, then that portion of my estate shall be held in trust until such time as said mortgage discharged in full.*

*Said mortgage is to be paid in the coin of my realm, which is love, cooperation, understanding, and forgiveness. If payments are missed, due to negative thought indulgence, receipt of the inheritance is postponed by virtue thereof.*

*However, this further proviso is hereby stipulated: Namely, that the mortgage, with any and all past interest, may be paid in full at any interest-bearing date. The time for such payment is NOW—in this moment of awakening.*

(Signed)    UNIVERSAL MIND, THE FATHER

## Your will to live

Have you been reading the universal will rightly? Do you know that its will for you is life and life more abundant? Have you accepted this will? Have you claimed this bequest to you by accepting your responsibility regarding your inheritance?

Dr. David Schwartz, in *The Magic of Psychic Power,* said, "More than half the people I talk to have written clearly defined plans for death. But not one percent have written clearly defined plans for life. A plan for death but no plan for life." [2]

Have you prepared your will—*your will for life?* Without question, a person should put his house in order for his loved ones before he makes his grand departure. But why not put your mental house in order for yourself and your loved ones while here on earth? Read the suggested

193

"will for living" declaration below, and then write it out in your own handwriting to make it your very own:

*I, as heir to the abundance of the universe, as recipient of infinite givingness, as one who has prospered in all ways, knowing the responsibility that rests upon me as one who measures the riches of life and being of sound mind, do hereby bequeath to the future days of my life the following riches that have been willed to me by Universal Mind:*

*I will to tomorrow—by being conscious today that I am the recipient of untold riches of body, mind, and spirit—the attitude of a quiet but confident mind. I include in my will proper care for my body as the individualized temple of spirit.*

*I will to myself future happiness, knowing that it is born of today's beliefs and mental concepts. Aware that tomorrow's joy springs from today's seed, I plant today the seed of patience with myself, forgiveness of my past mistakes, willingness to learn, and perseverance in my own destiny.*

*To each of my brothers and sisters—and I claim kinship with all people everywhere, of all races, colors, and creeds—I bequeath an understanding heart, a generous mind, and a forgiving spirit.*

*To those who are close to me on the road of life, I will my appreciation, my support, my love to wipe out their heartache, and my hand to help them to achieve the heights they seek.*

*To all, both near and far, I bequeath my empathy, my blessings, and my understanding to lighten their problems.*

*To the world that men call inanimate, with its rolling hills, its towering mountains, its prairies, and its life-sustaining seas, I give back the great joy with which it nourishes my spirit, my mind, and my body.*

*This is my first and lasting will and testament. I hereto affix my Seal of Individuality upon this document, declaring it to be binding upon me, henceforth and forever.*

(Your signature) _____
Universal Life Individualized

Copy and sign the above document. Make it even more individualistic by adapting it to reflect your own uniqueness and the way you can share it best. Make this "first will and lasting testament" a declaration of acceptance of the good that the universal has already willed to you. Then read it over periodically to renew your awareness of the rich heritage that is yours.

## Reverse your will to go downhill

When your car is parked on a hill, it takes little effort to let the car roll downward. Likewise, it is easy to let life roll downhill. Once started, it seems to gather momentum as it goes farther and faster. Often the will is directed downward—downward toward failure, toward defeat, toward limitation, toward loneliness and inadequacy.

There is such a thing as a subconscious will to defeat. It occurs when the subconscious has been working on negative data and the autoprompter of the subconscious produces a negative feedback of failure thoughts, prompting life along paths of discouragement, lowered self-esteem, worry, and resentment. The phenomenon that results is a will to limitation. It must be supplanted with a will to achieve.

## Your autoprompter of the subconscious

Ask yourself these important questions. Have I willed death in the midst of life? Have I willed poverty in the midst of plenty? Have I willed loneliness in a universe of love? Have I willed failure in the very presence of success?

Dr. Arnold Hutchnecker, author of *The Will to Live,* tells of a man who came to him to be treated for peptic ulcers from which he had been suffering for many years. All he asked of life was to be rid of his ulcers. The doctor asked him, "Suppose you woke up tomorrow cured, what would you do?

"Why, I would enjoy life," the man said.

"How would you enjoy life?" the doctor countered.

"Why," the patient floundered, "I would enjoy it like other people." [3] He could not be more specific. He had no plan, no purpose, no dynamic desire to be well in order to accomplish something that motivated him.

It cannot be assumed that all people who are ill have a need for illness. It would be inaccurate to say that all people who are poor have a need for poverty. But it would not be false to say that many people have adjusted their lives to certain negative states of mind which outpicture as illness and poverty.

It has been found in psychosomatic medicine that people may build their lives around illness, due to certain needs and drives. In like manner, others may build their lives around poverty concepts. Once these concepts are imprinted on the film of mind, the subconscious keeps feeding them back for rerunning again and again.

A great deal is being said about lifting people out of poverty. From a mental cybernetics standpoint, it is more important to get poverty out of people. Negative ideas, false concepts, and wrong attitudes call for poverty as a peach seed calls for a peach tree or a kernel of corn calls for a cornstalk.

### Cybernetic aids to autoprompt the mind lifeward

**1.** Understand that the urge of life to express is the "will" of universal life to fulfill itself by means of you. Therefore, will power is native to you. It may be dissipated, it may be inhibited, it may be wrongly directed, or it may remain in a dormant state—but, wherever life is expressing, *will* exists.

**2.** Frank Channing Haddock, in *The Power of Will,* said: "Will always is concerned with action and without action there is no completed process of will." [4] Do you remember George, the dreamer of great dreams? He envisioned glorious schemes but lacked the perseverance to persist in those dreams. If you are to make your will power work for you, you must realize that as important as it is to picture mentally what you want, you must not become arrested at the level of the dream. There must be action to carry your dream to fulfillment.

**3.** Understand the difference between willing and wishing. William James said, "If with the desire there goes a sense that attainment is not possible, we simply wish." [5] For a sense of attainment, there must be a realization of the power you use. The one who realizes that he is immersed in power—a power that he did not create but that he is free to use to an unlimited degree—is no longer wishing for the good things of life. Rather, he is *willing* with a feeling of accomplishment.

**4.** In addition to a realization of ample power, there must be the understanding that the power itself is impartial. As water will quench thirst or drown one, as electricity will cook food or electrocute one, so the power of mind acts only as acted upon. If used negatively, it produces negative results.

**5.** A goal, a destination, is essential to achievement. Without a goal to reach, the law of mind has nothing to work upon. It has no purpose to fulfill. It cannot act until something has been initiated. You must establish the goal. You must select the prize.

What do you want to achieve? It is not enough to say, "I want to enjoy life like other people." If you want to be healthy, what are you going to do with your health? Have a motive that impels you! If you want wealth, what are you going to use it for? Lack of a dynamic goal is one of the major obstacles to the effective use of will power.

### How to make your will power work for you

Today in industry, computer-controlled machines are performing marvels of production. Without computerization, for example, the conventional die cutter spends 15 minutes out of every hour actually making cuts. The other 45 minutes are wasted measuring for the next cut and adjusting the cutting tool. But, with computer-controlled tools, measurements and adjustments are done automatically in a fraction of the time.

Of course, before a die can be fabricated on a computerized tool, instructions must be worked out by engineers and programmed onto cards or tapes. These cards prompt the tool in its job as it cuts and designs the die. How are the cards prepared? Stanley Englebardt describes this programming process in his book, *Computers:*

> Not long ago a group of production men attending a demonstration at a plant of United Aircraft watched in fascination as a complex helicopter gearbox cover was fabricated automatically from Autoprompt's 110-word lexicon. These words were put together into 180 one-line sentences—each sentence describing a particular segment of the production operation. . . . The sentences were fed into a computer which, within minutes, spewed out some 8,000 detailed tool path instructions. These were punched into paper tape and fed into a continuous-path milling machine. . . . Actual fabrication of the part took exactly one-fourth the time formerly required.[6]

### The self-prompting power of words

The astonishing things possible in this computer age are no more praiseworthy than the fantastic things possible to man's mind itself. And the parallels are of particular interest. The computer is activated by the power of the word—such as IBM's Autoprompt with its 110-word vocabulary. Similarly, the computerlike subconscious mind is activated by the power of man's word. His word is spoken verbally or silently through his attitudes, self-concepts, and opinions. With his attitudes and self-conceptions, man prompts the tools that cut the conditions and events of his external life.

It is because man's word carries power—it is because he can command and control the subconscious with what he affirms—that the mind-processing cards in this book are effective. They are a self-prompting or auto-prompting device with which you can guide the creative, fabricating tools of mind. And, once the data on the cards is fed into the inner mind, it will make the necessary calculations and adjustments to accomplish your heart's desire.

This leads to another fascinating parallel between man's mind and a computer. Only general directions were fed into the computer described by Englebardt above. The computer then took over and from 180 sentences produced 8,000 detailed answers. Similarly, the subconscious mind, activated by general instructions, can take over and create an intricate design of experiences that correspond with the general commands given.

*Of utmost importance, then, is what a person says and thinks about himself day in and day out.* Your daily thoughts are like the card that directs the die-cutting, continuous-path milling machine of the subconscious. What have you punched into the program card that controls your creativeness?

### How your word and your will structure your world

Your world is shaped and molded by your word. Your speaking, however, is far more than verbal expression. It is consciousness that speaks, and consciousness is a composite of both the conscious and subconscious levels of mind. For years you have been programming commands into the subconscious. If those commands have been indiscriminate and derogatory—and if they were never cancelled with countercommands—you may find that the subconscious speaks louder negatively than the conscious speaks positively. You may find yoursef impulsively denying the very thing your conscious word affirms.

The subconscious acts as a self-prompter until reset with new programming. For example, you may wish to affirm: "I am going to prosper this year." But from the subconscious comes the thought, "You are kidding yourself; you didn't prosper last year! The going has always been rough!" This negative rebuttal dominates your word, and this word molds the experience of your world.

## THE SUBTLE PHRASES OF UNGUARDED HABITS

Examine the programmed phrases that automatically prompt your thinking. What do you habitually affirm day after day? Do your words run something like this:

> I have always been unlucky.
> I don't have what it takes.
> I don't have sufficient schooling for a better job.
> I have always found it difficult to make friends.
> My life is a mess.
> I don't know what I want from life.
> I am too old to start now.
> I can't seem to do anything right.
> No one appreciates me.

Such statements about yourself are like the 180 sentences fed into the computer at a large aircraft factory. They trigger the creative mechanism which fills in the details and spews out countless experiences that conform to the general statements. If these statements have been predominantly negative over the years, it will take strong positive mental action to change their effects.

Margery Wilson, in her book *Kinetic Psycho-dynamics,* says: "Too many people are desperately working in one direction while their tongues are wagging in an opposite way . . . People speak in careless, unlovely, destructive ways and then seem surprised that good fortune eludes them." [7]

## THE GREAT POWER OF KEY WORDS

It only takes a few key words repeated over and over again to autoprompt the mind with commands that will control your life. Reportedly, there were only 110 words in IBM's Autoprompt computer language, yet in various combinations these few symbols can trigger thousands upon thousands of detailed instructions. So it is with the key words you use. If those key words are negative—

*I can't, I don't, I won't, I doubt if*—a frightful array of detailed experiences can pour forth. These negative statements form your "word," your consciousness, and that consciousness spews forth thousands of intricate instructions in regard to your world of experience.

For example, the salesman who entertains ideas of inadequacy and says, "I just don't have the confidence it takes," the businessman who feels defensive and says, "I never get a crack at the big deals," or the woman who feels ill at ease and says, "I don't have the poise to meet people"—all are programming general commands into the subconscious that will return countless experiences of limitation.

How can such self-prompting patterns be changed? How can the mind be reset with new programming? Here is where imagination and will power enter in. Using the tool of imagination, man must create a new image of himself, and, using the vise of will power, he must hold his attention on that new image until it permeates his consciousness. When it does, his self-prompting word will become positive and will produce creative experiences.

## When positive thoughts may become negative

Curiously, some of the autoprompting that man considers to be positive may actually produce negative results. Therefore, in resetting your mind, make sure you are using statements that are completely positive in their implications. One statement you must examine is the affirmation, "Things will turn out all right." It is well to believe that things will move toward a happy conclusion, but don't let the declaration that "things will be all right" be an excuse for letting them drift and neglecting to do the muscular. If the individual fails to take definite mental or physical action and just lets his life drift, he will be blown to and fro by the haphazard influences from his own past programming. Or, even more risky, he will be swayed by the directional force of other minds.

It is easy to travel the road of least resistance. It is easy to let the winds of mass thought be the directing force in life. Henry David Thoreau, in *Walden, or Life in the Woods,* writes of lying down in the bottom of his boat as it drifted upon the lake and, when it landed, of looking out to see where he was. Thoreau was speaking of the need to relax and to enjoy the simplicity of nature. He found contentment in the beauty of the clouds as they floated overhead. Relaxation is necessary therapy in the maintenance of peace of mind. However, in the total business of living, you cannot let your life drift and only periodically look out to see where you have landed. Too often the landing place will not be to your satisfaction. You are likely to land at the port of poverty or run aground on the reef of regret.

Another attitude of mind that may be masquerading as a positive statement is, "I'm going to try to do better tomorrow." Such a declaration eases the mind today, but it postpones action into the future—and the future has a way of always being tomorrow. Instead, affirm, "I can do better now!" Word your command as a fact, as a present reality to be experienced. Create the mental image, now, of the good you desire. The computer sentences written in Autoprompt language are statements of fact. They are present commands. They are not conditional statements predicated upon the future and modified by *ifs, whens,* and *buts.* A computer must have this kind of data to process. The subconscious mind, too, must have present data to trigger its creative mechanism. It is for this reason that the mind-processing cards in this book are stated in affirmative, present tense language. The statements on the cards are directions that you feed into the subconscious to initiate creative results, like the keypunch cards fed into the United Aircraft milling machine to implement the fabrication of the gearbox cover. Both sets of directions are in the present tense. Both are commands to be followed. They cannot be stated in the future tense.

I remember Howard. Howard was always saying, "I'm determined to do something about this tomorrow." In the ten years that I knew him, he was daily determined to change things the next day. The following day he would rant and rave about conditions and again declare that he was determined to do something about them. Determination to act the following day had become a way of life for Howard. I never actually knew what he was determined to do, but he was determined to do it tomorrow for the ten years I knew him—and he probably still is. However, determination for Howard never led to action, for his statements were not in the present tense. Each day he was determined to act tomorrow, and this seemed to satisfy him until the following day when once again he would declare his intentions for the future.

Examine the positive statements you are formulating about yourself and your life, and make sure you are not committing the mistake Howard did. Don't postpone results by injecting the future tense into your autoprompting. By the same token, don't let things drift by neglecting to do the muscular. Things *will* turn out all right, but the action that initiates a solution must be taken today.

## The importance of planning, acting and willing

There is power in determination when it is followed by action. A determination to do something about your life must be implemented with planning, and planning must lead to action. Dynamic planning springs from goals and purposes that spark the imagination. You are not here just to occupy a few cubic feet of space or recline in a contour chair or sleep on a posture-right mattress. You are here to express a purpose of grandeur and stature. You are here to fulfill the father's *will* for you—the good willed to you by universal mind, the parent cause of your life.

Plan your life with this magnificent heritage in mind. Let your imagination soar with the possibilities open to you. Use your imagination creatively to envision the goals you want to achieve. Then use the vise of will power to hold you to your purposes until the finished product appears.

Consider a finished product, such as a fine chair as it emerges from the manufacturing plant. The chair appears to be made of one large piece of wood. Actually, it is fabricated of many pieces that were carefully planned, shaped, and milled, and then joined together with epoxy. After the glue is applied, the item is placed in a vise and held securely until the separate pieces appear

203

to become one. If the pieces are not held together until this oneness takes place, the joints soon loosen and the chair falls apart.

The power of your will is like a vise. It holds you to your image, your ideals, your purposes, your goals and plans, until you become one with them. A lack of will power permits the image to fall apart before the goal has been realized. Firm resolve and determination are absolutely necessary in the act of reprogramming your mind for success.

## How to use willpower effectively

However, do not mistake firm resolve and determination for a stubborn stance of mind. Frank Channing Haddock, in *Power of Will,* states that "The man who really is firm is fixed in purpose, but he is willing to change his position when his purpose is thereby served. The stubborn man, however, is fixed only in position— he sticks to his position even if his purpose is imperilled and destroyed thereby." [8]

### HOW TO GET POSITIVE RESULTS

In putting your will power to work, follow these four safeguards and create results that are positive:

*First,* develop a strong will, a determination to achieve your goals. But remember that along with a firm resolve must go flexibility. You must be flexible enough to change your position when your goals are served thereby. Don't tie down the creative power of the subconscious to a fixed pattern of achievement. The stereotype of the successful man may not be the picture for you at all. Give your subconscious the latitude to fulfill your dreams in a unique, imaginative way.

*Second,* don't develop will power just to hold yourself to what you have been doing. You shall continue to do that anyway, with little effort. Once imagination becomes set, the will continues to work automatically until imagination resets the pattern. For the lower orders of life, set patterns of doing things have been evolved that bind the creature to instinctual repetition. In Chapter 6, remember, it was pointed out that although the nests birds build differ widely—from the swallow's mud home to the hummingbird's nest of plant down and spiderweb—birds of one species have evolved a set style that they reproduce year after year. Once imagination is set, automated will power produces a continual recurrence of experience. It is imagination, and not will power, that is the creative faculty of mind.

*Third,* don't doubt your freedom to change your mind. You have the free will to think differently than you have in the past. You are free to discard falsehoods and half-truths and create a new self-concept with the tools of imagination. To exercise this freedom, you must truly become a free thinker on the loose in the universe, and not just a loose thinker who is free to misuse his mind or a bound thinker who continues to think as he has thought.

*Fourth,* use Mental Data Processing Card No. 19 daily to strengthen your will power and hold yourself to the goals you wish to demonstrate:

With new freedom of thought, I now design the finished product I desire to demonstrate. I envision it so keenly that imagination keypunches its image vividly upon my mind. I now put will power to work, holding me to my desire and making me one with it. That desire prompts subconscious, creative action and impels me toward fulfillment.

*Mental Data Processing Card No. 19*

## CHAPTER SUMMARY OF POINTS TO PONDER

1. Right mental photography, with the camera of imagination, is essential to the demonstration of success. But once you have formed a vivid mental picture of what you want to be or do, the dynamic of will power must be employed to carry your demonstration to completion.

2. Imagination and will power are an inseparable team. Imagination determines the end result, while will maintains a true course toward its achievement.

3. The *will* of universal mind for you is life and life more abundant! You are the beneficiary of the universe in all its fullness of supply, wisdom, and power.

4. Due to your freedom, you can draw up a will that leads to greater happiness, success, and self-mastery, or you can will yourself experiences that lead downward toward failure and unhappiness.

5. A great deal has been said concerning the desirability of lifting people out of poverty. What really needs to be done is to lift poverty out of people. For poverty images, poverty concepts, and belittling beliefs *must* out-picture as impoverishment.

6. Due to autoprompting commands programmed into the subconscious, the individual often continues along a path predetermined by previously programmed material. Detailed experiences are spewed forth from basic concepts fed into the computer of subconscious mind.

. Your future is not predetermined if you exercise the free will that is inherently yours. You are free to think new concepts about yourself, but you must choose to exercise that freedom.

8. Your world of experience is the result of your will working upon your word. Your word is your consciousness. It is a composite of the many desires, thoughts, ideas, attitudes, and impressions that you entertain daily.

9. A strong will is a firmness of resolve. However, do not mistake resolve for stubbornness. Be flexible enough to change if your purpose will be served thereby.

10. Will power is a holding power, not a forming power. Its function is to hold in place what the conscious mind designs and forms.

# CHAPTER ELEVEN

## How to Live A High Voltage Life Through Mental Cybernetics

As I looked at Hilda across the desk, she reminded me of a 20-watt light bulb that was about to go out. Hilda was still young—possibly in her late 30's—but she seemed much older. It was plain that life was a drag. Her walk, her talk, and the way she dressed reflected what might be described as a very low-voltage life.

Hilda was plain and she knew it. She was bored with life and she showed it. She had not married and had long since given up hope in that area. As we talked, it became obvious that her self-confidence was practically nil.

Hilda worked as a filing clerk. From her attitude toward her job, it seemed she derived very little excitement from it or from the people with whom she worked. Her social life was non-existent.

"What do I have to live for?" she sighed. "My day has become a monotonous routine of getting up in the morning, eating breakfast alone [Hilda had been living by herself since her mother passed away a year before], going to work, and coming home in the evening to prepare dinner alone. By that time I'm so tired that I watch television only a little while before going to bed." The next morning, the dull routine started all over again. She would rise with her 20-watt light and sally forth to illumine a dim corner in the office where she worked.

**Boredom breeds low-voltage living**

Hilda had come to my office seeking release from

monotony. That she needed help was obvious. I almost found myself wondering how she had worked up enough energy or interest to get there. But the spark of life is tenacious, and while a spark exists, a flame is potential— as I was to learn later.

However, it was clear that the batteries of her mind were badly in need of recharging. The light of interest was burning low. Her whole attitude was one of "Why go on?" I am sure she had never contemplated suicide, but she was searching for some purpose and point to life.

"Have you had a physical examination lately?" I inquired. It turned out that she had one recently and that the doctor had found nothing wrong from a medical viewpoint. On her own she had decided to take vitamins. That was an aid, but it could do only so much.

Since nothing was wrong at the physical level, it left the mental level to consider. Her main ailment at that level was the boredom into which life had settled. Boredom accounted for Hilda's listlessness, for her lack of vitality, for her chronic tiredness, and for her hopeless attitude.

## How to recharge the batteries of your mind

If "you are the light of the world," as a great teacher of long ago said, what happens to dim that light? What happens to those whose lights are hardly lit, as was the case of Hilda?

Individuals do display a vast range of manifest power. There are those whose light may be likened to a 20-watt bulb, some glow like a 40-watt light, while others radiate more like 60 or 100 watts. As voltage power ranges upward in brilliancy to bulbs that can light a baseball field, so there are high-powered personalities that illuminate entire fields of endeavor. A few become great floodlights of history and illumine the world.

Does this range of brilliancy happen by chance? Or can it be cultivated? Can a person somehow be recharged and raised in brilliancy? The answer is yes! There are certain qualities and attitudes that charge the mind, causing it to glow brighter. There are certain data that can be used to recharge the batteries of the mind when thinking becomes dull and lifeless.

## How alive are you?

Many centuries ago, the prophet Isaiah implored, "Restore me to health and make me live." [1] Psychosomatic medicine today advocates a train of thought just the reverse of this: "Make me alive that I might be restored to health." Health of body, of mind, and affairs is dependent upon the degree of one's "aliveness." Aliveness is a state of being that is superior to health. Health will flow from it, of course, but aliveness must exist first.

There are many who try to reverse this process with the belief that "if I had health, wealth, and an abundance of things, I could enjoy life." *But aliveness comes first, then health, wealth, and an abundance of things.*

### Your level of awareness

Out of man's degree of livingness comes the assessment of outer effects and conditions. For you, this means that the thrill you get from outer events will be measured by your degree of inner aliveness. Therefore, pause and ask yourself: "How alive am I?" Or, because aliveness is a matter of awareness, "How aware am I?" How *aware* are you of the wonders of nature, of the break-throughs in science, and of the awesome adventures awaiting man in space? How alive are you to innovations in your profession or endeavors that occupy your attention. Individuals may be alive in different ways. The geologist is fascinated by oil shales and domes, the botanist is radiant over taxonomy, the architect glows over Doric columns, the poet lights up when talking about iambic meter and blank verse. Each in his own field may be interested in a different thing. Yet it gives him that aliveness which prevents boredom and is conducive to success, happiness, fulfillment, and satisfaction.

### How to overcome the mental depressant of monotony

One of the major mental depressants of life is monotony. The life dictionary defines *monotony* as "continuity of one unvarying tone or sound; sameness or want of variety." Monotony does not imply the lack of thought, but rather, the repetition of thought. Like a small train at a county fair that makes a circle of the same scenery over and over, so the mind that travels the same small circuit of thought sees the same things with each recurring day. When the mind becomes habituated to mental states that are going no place to do nothing, monotony sets in.

The depressive effect of boredom upon the mind and body cannot be overemphasized. It is recognized that fatigue, many times, is caused by monotony. Possibly you may recall a time when, seemingly exhausted, you were unexpectedly invited by a friend to go fishing, hunting, or to a baseball game. Your tiredness vanished like magic. And what girl has not come home weary from work or shopping, convinced that the only thing she wanted to do was to eat and go to bed, when a telephone call suddenly banished all fatigue. The boy friend picked her up, and she had quite enough energy to dance half the night.

Elmer Wheeler, in *How to Sell Yourself to Others,* tells of research conducted with students at Georgia Tech in Atlanta a number of years ago which showed that fatigue is mainly boredom. He states, "Students were kept awake for several days. Even with no sleep for three or four days these students kept up a high energy level—but, only as long as their interest was kept alive." [2] Individuals become chronically tired when the mind isn't going any place. When the mind is alert and alive, physical fatigue is held to a minimum.

J. B. Rhine, in his experiments at Duke University with extra-sensory perception, found that monotony and boredom were definite factors in poor psi-scoring. The subject who became fatigued with monotony fell below the chance level in the extrasensory tests. On the other hand, interest, excitement, and enthusiasm were vital factors in maintaining a high-scoring level.[3] It is clear that when boredom occurs, not only does physical fatigue set in, but mental and extrasensory powers are dimmed as well. The person who is alive mentally and "going places," is also alive physically.

## The subtle effects of negative adaptation

If the temperature of a room falls gradually, a person fails to notice the change for some time. When taxes are increased gradually, first in one category and then in another, the increased burden is not perceived immediately. It may take some time before the individual realizes that a change has taken place.

The same is true of life. The temperature of living may decline so gradually that the individual is not aware of what has happened, of why it happened, or even when. This was true for Hilda's case in the first part of this chapter. Life had settled down to a sameness by imperceptible degrees. She was not aware that anything was wrong until it was all wrong. She was not able to pinpoint a particular time when the light of interest began to flicker. Such is the power of negative adaptation. The mind becomes conditioned gradually to things as they are.

One by one, interests had been slipping away from Hilda. Friends she knew when younger had married. Some had moved away. Some were preoccupied with their own families. Interest in life dipped even lower when her mother passed away. It left a large, vacant place in Hilda's life that she failed to fill with new interests. Hilda did love to read, and being introspective, she spent many happy hours daydreaming. There is nothing wrong with daydreaming, up to a point. It can provide a necessary escape from dull routine, but it should not become a substitute for reality.

In spite of her inclination to daydream, Hilda did not find such fantasy to be a satisfactory substitute for real experiences. Neither the inner dream content of her mind, nor the outer content of her life, was satisfying to her. She was not the type to withdraw further into a phantasy-land of unreality. Rather, she was seeking a better alignment with the outer world of real experience. She was seeking new interests that would raise her mental voltage power.

211

# The driving electric impulse of excitement

The mental windows through which the individual looks out upon his world are unique. They are designed and built by his own consciousness—by the data with which he has previously programmed his subconscious. Thus, each person views life in his own special way. This same thing happens when a group of people look through an actual window. Each one construes differently the scene he beholds. One may view the land spreading out before him as a farm. Another may see it as an excellent place for a subdivision. Still another may view the scene as the subject for a painting. Each person, although looking through the same window at the same physical scene, sees it with different mental eyes.

When monotony sets in, it is not so much the outer scene that needs changing, but the mental eye which beholds the scene. Interest springs more from an inner attitude of excitement over life than from outer circumstances. Hilda had lost that inner attitude of excitement. Thus, it was not the outer view that needed changing but her inner perception of that view. She needed the excitement of new ideas—ideas that would act as electrical impulses to give greater light to her life.

Hilda was desperately in need of a love affair—a love affair with life. She had become a self-imprisoned system. She needed to break free mentally and embrace interests that would spark her mind. Her monotonous life had produced what may be described as battle fatigue. What she needed was a mental electric shock to get her life moving again. She needed aliveness. As J. C. Street puts it in *Hidden Ways Across the Threshold,* "Live thought is like lightning. It dazzles the eye and strikes the heart . . . The decadence or total loss of enthusiasm is the greatest calamity that can overtake human life." [4]

# Your gift of life

I asked Hilda to think back to the many presents she had received through the years—at Christmas time, for birthdays, graduations, and special occasions. I asked her to select the most meaningful gift she had been given in the past. She thought for a moment, finding it difficult to decide. Finally she said, "A watch I received from my parents upon graduation from high school."

"Try to recapture now the great joy you felt when the gift was presented. Try to regain the thrill that ran through you as you opened it," I said, for I wanted her to generate that same excitement for another gift I was about to mention.

Now I asked Hilda to picture in mind the most wonderful gift that she could picture herself receiving through all the years to come. I said, "Imagine that the wealthiest person in the whole world wants to buy you a present. Money is no object. He loves you very much. There is nothing that he wouldn't do for you. Your happiness is the most important thing in the world to this person. What would be your request?"

Hilda's bewilderment seemed to say that she would not be able to choose easily. It was a question I really didn't expect her to answer, for I already had a reply. "Would you believe that you have already received the greatest of all gifts? It is the most precious of all! It is the gift that makes all other things meaningful. It is the gift that embraces the potential of all wealth, all love, all wisdom, and all power. It is the *gift of life*."

I asked Hilda to mentally picture a large box, beautifully wrapped and tied with colorful ribbons. The label on the box reads, "Your Gift of Life."

I asked Hilda to contemplate that gift, letting her mind expand with the limitless potentials the gift holds— the potentials of growth, discovery, learning, adventure, and experiences ad infinitum. I reminded her of the thrill and excitement she had felt for the watch received many years before. "Re-create that feeling now—only double it, triple it—and let it animate your being. Glow with the pleasure of enjoying the greatest gift in the world! Radiate with the joy of unwrapping and using the wonders of *your gift of life*."

### How to unwrap the gift of life

Hilda was asked to think about the thrill of this gift-package for a few days and to answer a number of questions that we would discuss at her next visit. These are the questions I asked her. Consider them now and answer them for yourself:

1. Where is the gift of life? Is it in your environment—in the outer world of form and effect? Or is it within you—in your creativeness and ability to cause things to be?

2. What is the gift of life? Is it happiness, wealth, love, and understanding? Is it a special talent or a unique ability? Or, possibly, is the gift of life multiple burdens, unhappiness, sorrow, poverty, illness, and heartbreak?

3. Is your gift box smaller than that which life has given someone else? Do you feel that yours is an inferior $1.98 present, while another has been given a million-dollar present? Or can you believe that life has given you an infinite potential, presenting you a blank check that you are free to fill in according to your consciousness?

4. How has your gift come to you? Do you feel that yours has come by slow freight with extra-handling charges, while the gift of another came prepaid and special delivery?

5. Have you failed to open your gift yet? If so, what are you waiting for?

6. Did you know that if you are to untie the ribbons on the gift of life and enjoy its content, some special-handling directions must be followed? Careless unwrapping and thoughtless use of the gift can damage the contents.

7. Now, consider that the ribbons holding down the lid of the box are thoughts—your thoughts about yourself. Thoughts that are negative, belittling, self-pitying, dull, and self-defeating tend to constrict the bow into a tight, stubborn knot that will not open. On the other hand, positive, confident thoughts about yourself tend to untie the bow and release your gift of life. Stop now and make a list of positive attitudes you should entertain in order to unwrap the wonders of life awaiting you.

8. As an eighth point, I gave Hilda a special affirmation similar to Mental Data Processing Card No. 20 that she was to repeat twice daily until her return visit. Use this card yourself for daily mental processing. Let it help you unwrap life's gift to you.

The life that pulsates through me now and makes me alive and aware is the most precious of all gifts. As I contemplate the wonder of being alive, the very thrill of it fills me with excitement. There is so much to be done! So much to be experienced! I am eager to be up and doing—to accomplish more, to learn more, to be more! I am on my way now!

*Mental Data Processing Card No. 20*

## The land of beginning again

When Hilda returned for our next visit, I seemed to detect a newness about her that I had not seen previously. She seemed much younger than she had appeared the week before. She said to me, "You know, I have been thinking a great deal about my life, and I have been studying the points you asked me to consider. I know that changes are going to take place in my life. I feel that this is a new beginning for me."

Finding a better land, a land of beginning again, has been a dream shared by people of all times and of all climes. Does this land belong to some other world, to a hereafter, or to a here and now? Is it an external realm or an internal region of mind? The answer is that it belongs to this world right now but that it is an internal realm. People are very conscious of where they live externally. In answer to the question, "Where do you live?" the automatic reply is a house number, a street, and a city—data describing an external realm. The question never evokes the automatic response that "I live in

215

the Land of Loneliness," or "I live on the Fairway of Faith." Yet, such a response would be more accurate. It would describe the actual internal realm discussed in Chapter 4.

Hilda opened her purse and took out her replies to the series of questions I had posed at our first meeting. In answer to the query, "Where is the gift of life?", Hilda acknowledged that it was within her own awareness of it. And, in response to the second question, "What is the gift of life?" she replied with the conclusion that it was freedom from loneliness, the absence of self-depreciation, and the acceptance of happiness and love. She was starting to find her land of beginning again. She was willing to accept the idea that her land need no longer lie barren or that it need bear only the harvest of yesterday.

In the science of mental cybernetics, man's life may be defined as a composite of where he lives, what he eats, and what he breathes—mentally, of course. Where do you live in terms of consciousness? What are the thoughts, ideas, and attitudes feeding your mind? What kind of mental atmosphere do you breathe? You know that spoiled food may give you ptomaine poisoning, but do you know that negative mental food will poison every situation, every relationship of life? What is the mental atmosphere that you breathe daily? You would not walk into a room filled with deadly gas fumes, would you? Be as cautious of the thought atmosphere to which you expose yourself! Also, watch your own mental environment! Avoid inhaling an atmosphere of defeat, unworthiness, and self-limitation that may poison your success, peace of mind, health, and happiness.

Men landing on the Moon must carry with them their own life-giving oxygen. They cannot live in the lifeless atmosphere that they find there. Hilda had been living in a lifeless atmosphere of self-depreciation, boredom, and lovelessness. She was in need of oxygen—she needed to breathe the fresh air of life—and this she was ready to do. "But," she asked, "where do I begin?"

**How to start where you now stand**

I asked Hilda if she could accept the idea that she has

received the same gift of life that all others have received. Could she believe that she had not been shortchanged? "You must see," I explained, "that you have received the same gift of life that seeks expression through all people and forms. Life is an infinite potential and, as such, presents to each one a blank check which he is free to fill in according to his own evaluation."

"But," Hilda quickly interposed, "what of those who seem to be behind the eight ball at birth?"

I explained that life is still potentially a blank check. Some figures may have been filled in at birth. Some people may be born crippled or handicapped by environment. From a mass-mind standpoint, preliminary evaluations may have been set by the society into which an individual is thrust. However, from a present-position standpoint, those evaluations are subject to change. By his own efforts, man can alter the figures that environment and heredity may have scribbled on his blank check of life. The value of that check is limitless!

However, to utilize that check in practical terms of success and creative fulfillment, you must start where you stand. It does no good to complain because you are not standing elsewhere. It is futile to lament because you cannot see other scenery from where you stand. What you must do is move forward step by step from where you now are to where you want to be. Until you take the first step, your vision remains limited. You cannot see life from any position other than that which you occupy.

I asked Hilda if the teacher had ever made her stand in the corner as a child. She replied that she had. "What could you see from that position? Could you," I suggested, "see the rest of the room or anyone in the room?" Her reply was as expected. Her view was limited to the corner in which she stood.

I explained that life was like that. From where she stood, she could not possibly see anyone or anything that was beyond her range of vision. Thinking of life as a large room with a multitude of things that are possible to view, the individual can only enjoy that which is within his range of vision. Likewise, the multitude of things potential to man become actual only as he changes

217

his position relative to the room of life. To change, you must start where you stand. This is not to say that you must stay where you stand. But you cannot miraculously find yourself elsewhere until you take your first step. Movement must begin where you are right now. Things will look different the moment you lift up your eyes. Things will be different the moment you step forward.

**Look up from the place where you are**

I told Hilda the story of a certain man who shined shoes. His shop was in the basement of a building that had one small window which looked out at the street level. All day long as he shined shoes, he glanced out the window and saw nothing but the feet of passersby. And, when he went home at night, he found himself staring down at the feet of those who walked along with him. His whole consciousness was preoccupied with shoes. Such is the power of habit.

Of course, here is nothing wrong with shining shoes. To change his consciousness, it was not necessary for this man to stop doing that which provided him a livelihood. It was only necessary for him to look up while pursuing his trade.

Look up from the place where you are! Even if you remain in the same environment, there is much, much more to be seen if you will only look up. Raise your eyes from where you are and you will see yourself in a new light. You will begin to perceive that your life has greater meaning than you have previously believed. You will start to draw a larger circle around yourself, and, as you continue to look up, this circle will become larger and larger until the place where you are is no longer able to contain you! You will overflow it! As you overflow it through greater service, through greater love and understanding, and through enthusiasm and expectancy, your world will become brighter and you will be on your way to high-voltage living.

This happened to a man of ancient times. He and his kinsman agreed to separate, each going his own way. After he had separated himself from previous conditions, he was at a loss as to what to do. Then the words came to him, "Lift up your eyes and look from the place where you are, northward and southward and eastward and westward; for all the land which you see I will give to you. . . . Arise, walk through the length and breadth of the land, for I will give it to you." [5]

This was what life said to Abram as he separated himself from Lot. This is what life is saying to you: "Look up from the place where you are mentally, for all the land which you are able to traverse in mind can be yours." But the starting point is "Look up!"

## Learn to walk on mental tiptoe

"Look up and learn to walk on mental tiptoe," I advised Hilda. What does walking on mental tiptoe mean? To be on tiptoe is *to be aroused, alert, to stand so as to see better, to stand expectantly, eagerly*. To be mentally expectant and eager is to stretch to see bigger and better potentialities for yourself.

What do you expect from life? Do you believe that tomorrow will be better than today—that the next five years will be better than the past five? Or are you like the woman who was overheard to say, "Beginning Monday, I will have a full week's vacation—the first in three years—and I suppose it will rain all week!"

Many people expect the worst, and they are rarely disappointed. They are conditioned to accept only what has already happened in the past, and, since this is their level of expectancy, they continue to experience what has happened before. The person who has had an unhappy life expects it to continue. This had been the situation for Hilda. The same things had been happening day after day for many years. The track of unhappy, monotonous experiencing was well oiled, and traveling was easy. Now, for changed results, new tracks must be laid, new data processed, and new habits formed. How was this to be done?

I explained to Hilda that the mind and body operate as a team. While the mind is the conscious boss and director, the body has a reactive influence upon the mind. For example, when the individual is mentally depressed, the body is likely to slouch. The physical man takes on the manifest evidence of mental depression. His face becomes downcast. His body lacks vitality, and his gait becomes slow. In turn, the physical slump in his posture will have a reactive influence upon his mind. He looks as he feels, and he feels as he looks.

Since the mind's eye perceives what it is conditioned to experience, and since her conditioning had been of long standing, I suggested to Hilda a dual attack upon her problem, placing equal emphasis upon physical conditioning and right thinking. She was instructed to pay particular attention to the following steps as she began the work of restyling her life. Each step is an exercise in the art of standing on mental tiptoe. You, too, will find these exercises effective in programming the body and mind for success.

## A PROGRAM TO STAND ON MENTAL TIPTOE

*First,* give particular attention to your posture. Get a full-length mirror, if you do not already have one, and stand in front of it morning and evening. As you stand before it, mentally picture yourself growing another inch or two. Gaze in the mirror until you can mentally see your image rising. Expand the mind as you stretch the body. You may not actually grow taller, but you will rise on mental tiptoe and become more alert, expectant, and aware of bigger and better potentials for yourself.

*Second,* observe the way you walk. Cultivate a regal movement. Move with pride at each step. Let your arms swing freely by your side as you stride along. Practice this physically, and then sit down and practice a regal stance in your imagination. Then arise again and walk as you have pictured yourself walking in mind. Continue with this exercise until you can truthfully say, "I walk with the stride of a confident person."

*Third,* increase the speed of your gait. Without losing the charm of your movement, lengthen your step slightly and increase the speed of your stride. This will impart the impression, first to yourself and then to others, that you are going someplace. Men, observing this confidence, may wonder where you are going and start following you. (Hilda smiled at the idea of men following her, but she got the point.)

*Fourth*, if there are factors about your physical appearance that could be improved—if you are underweight or overweight or if your wardrobe is too drab—do something about it! Hilda, who was slightly overweight, needed to start a sensible plan of dieting. Also, she needed to buy herself some new clothes—preferably bright colors. To commit herself to a new wardrobe, and because she could afford it, I suggested that she call some service agency and let them cart off the present contents of her closet.

## How to recharge your life with enthusiasm

In addition to the physical correctives man can practice to influence the mind, attention must be given to the mind's dominion over the body. The mind and body are a team, and working with one alone will not suffice. If the mind lacks enthusiasm for life, it will cause the body to age prematurely. If the body is allowed to slump or become overweight, it will harm the mental image.

Enthusiasm is life's tonic. Literally, enthusiasm means divine inspiration or possession by divine drive. It springs from the word *entheos*—to be inspired by life. To have enthusiasm is to be intoxicated with life. To drink the heady wine of enthusiasm is to add joy, beauty, vitality, and richness to each day.

Enthusiasm is the magic potion that adds to all things. Lack of enthusiasm leads to monotony, and monotony causes much of man's physical weariness. It depresses the body and sets up negative vibrations, causing the whole physical system to register at a low key.

The feeling of zest you need to generate and maintain through life is like that of a small boy as he goes off with his gang to a ball game or to the swimming pool. He is truly walking on mental tiptoe. There is anticipation, excitement and enthusiasm. He is going someplace to do something important, and he knows it.

Success or failure in life is determined more by man's E.Q. (his enthusiasm quotient) than by his I.Q. (his intelligence quotient). A person may succeed in life

221

without being the most intelligent person around if he has boundless enthusiasm. Zest for living keeps the gauge of experience high. That same gauge dips low when monotony is allowed to set in. There are degrees of aliveness and lifelessness, and many people slip toward the lifeless end of the gauge of experience. They are deader than they realize. It is easy to die young. For such a victim was the tombstone carved that reads: "Died at thirty; buried at seventy." It is easy to sleep. When enthusiasm wanes and inertia sets in, death claims man long before he stops breathing.

### Mental exercises to complement physical ones

To complement and reinforce the physical exercises I had recommended to Hilda, I proposed some mental ones to recharge her life with enthusiasm and make for high-voltage living. Again, you may make use of them yourself:

*First,* you must develop confidence in life—a basic trust and a firm faith that life is meaningful. There must be faith in a power that is greater than yourself—a power that is orderly, dependable, and adequate at all times. You must realize that this power is yours, that it is the very essence of life. You cannot live severed—in consciousness—from this power, just as a tree cannot live severed from the soil that sustains it. When a tree is cut, it begins to die. When your life is cut off—in consciousness—from the source from which you spring, you begin to die. To have interest, to be enthusiastic, to feel that life is meaningful, your life must be rooted in something that gives it meaning.

*Second,* love is essential to an increase in aliveness. Every person has the need to be needed and the need to give. It is not possible to live vitally without love. Existence is possible, but not life! It is therefore essential for the individual to find ways of caring—outlets for love. A person who has stopped caring gradually deteriorates. It shows up in his attitude, in his lack of vitality, in his manner of dress, and in personal care.

*Third,* a purpose is vital to high-voltage living. The individual must have someplace to go. The subconscious works upon the data that you provide—it accepts the mental food you feed it—and from this flows the distillation called experience. Good cannot consistently flow from inconsistent interests and actions. A wobbly frame of mind must produce wobbly results. A goal is essential to keep the mind on course.

*Fourth,* regardless of your work—whether you are a lawyer, teacher, actor, singer, salesman, clerk, mechanic, doctor—you must live with the pulsebeat of expectation. You must keep alive the expectation of the *more* that is yet to be. You must lift your head and look forward to future attainment, walking always on mental tiptoe. You increase the figure on your blank check-of-life with your enthusiasm, vision, and expectation. Start building that feeling of expectation now by using Mental Data Processing card No. 21 morning and evening.

I now look up from the place where I am. I stand on mental tiptoe and stretch my consciousness until I see a greater potential for myself. I anticipate the fulfillment of that potential with enthusiasm and eagerness. I see myself filling and overflowing that potential and moving forward to even greater things.

*Mental Data Processing Card No. 21*

## CHAPTER SUMMARY OF POINTS TO PONDER

1. How alive are you? Out of the aliveness of your mind flow exciting situations; out of its lifelessness flow dull situations.
2. Monotony is existence at one unvarying tone of consciousness—a state that depresses the mind, the body, and the affairs of life.
3. The cells of the body march to the tune of consciousness. Thus, a monotonous tune produces fatigue and depression.

223

4. To cultivate live thought is to incorporate new ideas into the storehouse of mind, breaking the hold of monotonous, crystalized attitudes.

5. Live thought taps the potentials of the gift of life you have been given—that wondrous gift that is especially wrapped for you, imprinted with your own uniqueness, and bears your name.

6. Your gift is an infinite potential—a blank check —awaiting your evaluation and signature.

7. You must look up from the place where you are if you are to increase the figures on your check-of-life, for, what your mind's eye perceives, you are conditioned to experience.

8. To enter the land of beginning again, you must start where you stand and take the first step forward.

9. To see more than you now experience, you must stand on mental tiptoe and stretch to behold a bigger and better potential for yourself.

10. Enthusiasm is the battery that gives a charge to life. Enthusiasm increases the vibratory rate of the mind and makes for high-voltage living.

# CHAPTER TWELVE

*How to Program Your
Mind for Success With
Mental Cybernetics*

The science of cybernetics plays a vital role in our lives today. At the present time, every person, from the moment of birth to the final exit, becomes a part of the memory bank of one or more digital computers either as a name, a number, or a statistic—or, possibly, all three. Computer programming reaches into every area of living, and this reach will become more extensive in the future.

Along with the time-saving blessings of computerization go some disadvantages. There are those who resent being reduced to a code number and run through an impersonal machine. The computer authority, Stanley L. Englebardt, tells of an eccentric woman who was found mutilating her utility and department store keypunch cards. It was discovered that she took a nail file and made extra holes so the computer kicked out the card when it was being processed. When asked for a reason for her behavior, the woman replied: "To confuse those brain machines good and proper! I'm not going to have any electronic gadget peep into my bedroom. I'm going to nip this automation thing in the bud." [1]

But automation is here to stay—and not only to stay, but to increase. Automation speeds progress, enabling man to do more work in less time. In industry, man has created machines that activate machines that activate machines! This is automation.

# How to avoid becoming an automaton

The dictionary defines an automaton as: 1. *A thing regarded as capable of spontaneous motion or action;* 2. *A self-moving machine, especially one which imitates the motions of men, birds, etc.;* 3. *A person who behaves mechanically, especially one following a routine without active intelligence.*

It is to the credit of man that he is able to create a machine that imitates himself, but it is not to man's credit when he imitates a machine. Yet, due to the nature of the subconscious mind—to retain and reproduce that which is stored in its memory bank—the individual becomes programmed in mechanical ways. The trick is to program the mind with success images that will produce, mechanically, the happiness and achievement desired.

# How to use your UMI card

In designing and building the electronic computer, man has indeed created a machine that imitates himself. His subconscious mind, like the memory bank of a computer, is a storehouse of memory. In it are stored not only data relating to his own personal history but principles drawn from all the sciences. Like a computer, the subconscious is triggered into action by the commands given to it. It obeys. It reasons from premise to conclusion. It produces answers.

Man's individual subconscious mind is like an auxiliary computer in a large computer complex. That complex is universal mind. It is the cosmic computer that contains all wisdom, power, and know-how. Being one with the total complex, man's individual power reaches into the infinite.

What triggers the creative action of the subconscious? What sets the auxiliary computer in motion? It is man himself. Man's state of consciousness is like an IBM card. When that card is fed into an electronic computer, things begin to happen. For example, take an IBM payroll card with its configuration of key punch holes. Those holes describe a specific employee and give personal data about his status, his pay rate, tax deductions, withholding, and the hours worked. When this card is run through a computer, his pay for the period is figured and a paycheck is spewed forth. When it comes to the cosmic computer of universal mind, man himself is the keypunch card. Stamped upon him are stylized markings (consciousness) that make him unique and distinct. He might be termed a UMI card—UNIVERSAL MIND INDIVIDUALIZED!

You are such a UMI card. You are a personalized expression of life. And the unique punches on your mental card give you an identity that cannot be confused with any other person who has ever lived. You are a representation of universal data that can never be duplicated. That representation which you are is of unique value. It is a special, perfect part of the total scheme. It has distinct talents and abilities that are essential to the whole. This is your claim to greatness! This is your area of contribution that makes you an indispensable individual. This is what programs you for success!

However, the unique and special UMI card that you are becomes subject to the forces around you. At birth, you enter into mental atmospheres and relationships that stamp new data upon your individuality. In the process of relating to society and the environment around you, your self-image is altered. You are very much like the little old lady with the nail file who altered and mutilated her IBM billing cards, changing the original data on them. The uniquely perfect and special person you are becomes altered to the extent that you corrupt your original self-image. Through ignorance of the real self, you build an assumed self—an ego self. Chances are that your assumed self is not demonstrating the confidence and success potential to you.

If the changes punched in your UMI card by ignorance, environment, and conditioning are negative—if alterations have been made that classify the assumed self as inadequate, incapable, unwise, and uncreative—the auxiliary computer of your subconscious must process negative data and produce negative results for you. Unlike the computer that rejected the little old lady's altered IBM card, your subconscious computer does not mechanically reject false self-image data. Therefore, your self-image must be constructive and based upon the accurate conception that you are an individualization of something universal.

## The nature of universal mind

What is the nature of this universal mind that has given rise to the individualization of mind that you are? I remember a woman saying to me, "I don't care about the nature of the universe; I only want to know how to get along better in life."

To get along better is a desire basic to the heart. But, to demonstrate better results, a person must know the nature with which, and from which, he has to work. It is unreasonable to believe that the individual is a product of anything other than universal mind—just as it would be unreasonable to believe that an electric light is a product of anything other than the principle of electricity. You are an individualization of the principle of mind. As an apple comes out of an apple tree, so have you come out of the tree of mind.

Hence, the properties of universal mind are present within the seed of the self that you are. What are the properties and potentialities in the seed? No imagination is capable of encompassing in detail all the qualities, powers, and potentialities that constitute the nature of universal mind. However, from scientific observation, certain broad categories can be identified. One self-evident property is creativeness. The display of unlimited power is also quite evident. Wisdom and knowledge are certainly properties of the universal cause of things. Opulence, abundance, and givingness cannot be denied. Evident also are orderliness, harmony, dependability, and the operation of immutable laws. Accepting these properties as the data or facts of universal mind leads to the conclusion that individualizations of that mind partake of these same properties. And, certainly, such potentialities program the individual for success. How can man then, as universal mind individualized, fail when creativeness, unlimited power, wisdom, opulence, and harmony are originally programmed into his being? He can fail only to the extent that his thoughts alter or ignore that original program!

## Your use of the cosmic computer

You use the cosmic computer of mind to process the kind of life that the data of your thoughts demand. You individually represent life according to the dominant qualities of your mind. Life, as givingness, as intelligence, as creativeness, as orderliness and harmony, is individually channeled by means of you. Your use of universal powers and attributes is screened through your level of awareness.

Therefore, the same universal computer that processes wealth for one will produce poverty for another. Or, the computer that programs health, happiness, and personal mastery for one, will spew forth a program of illness, discouragement, and defeat for another. This is not because the cosmic computer of mind favors one over another, but solely because of the personalized mental data each feeds into the subconscious mind. If the self-image inherent in the original UMI (UNIVERSAL MIND INDIVIDUALIZED) card is not altered and mutilated by negative conditioning, success must manifest itself.

## Your program of life

What does the mental program of your life call for? Does the data with which you program your mind call for happiness, wisdom, and success? You cannot expect to receive from life that which is not included in your thought processing.

"But," you may counter, "if the universal drama of life calls for success, why do I witness so many failure performances? Why doesn't man experience the original play that universal life intends for him? Why do things turn out so differently?"

You may argue that when you attend a stage play and are handed a program showing the author, the director, the actors, and characters, you expect the plot to be followed. After you settle yourself comfortably and the

229

lights are dimmed, you would be surprised if the play turned out to be entirely different from that for which the program calls.

In your personal drama of life, however, you may be experiencing something quite opposite to what is intended in the original script. If so, it is likely that you are ignorant of the original program. The person who is unaware of the potentials of power, joy, success, and creativeness written into life's program for him can scarcely take advantage of them. The universal potentials within you are screened and limited by your level of awareness of them. Hence, the original script turns out differently than intended.

## The success drama of life in cybernetics

What you do to the original script for life's drama is one and the same with what you do to the original UMI card issued to you by the infinite. You limit and alter it with your perception. You distort it with your ignorance of self. You modify it with your lack of awareness. You personalize the drama of life with the self-image you have assumed.

*The science of mental cybernetics describes the drama of life in terms of three acts.* The *first act* of that drama, which portrays the infinite cause from which you came, may be obscured from you by the mists of ignorance. You may have no knowledge of the vastness of the creative power that has pushed itself forth through the eons, finally culminating in man and self-awareness.

You may only be aware of the *second act*—the place you are now. Act two is the mental level where you are now using or misusing the potentials of mind power you inherited from the universal. In all likelihood, you are asleep to your uniqueness.

*Act three* is the stage you aspire to reach. In this scene you awaken to the infinite potentials of creativeness and success intended for you from the beginning. With a new awareness of self, you discard all false data and the original, perfect self-image expresses itself. In Act three, you discard the negative conditioning of environment and live the life of freedom and success inherent in the universal cause from which you came.

Let us imagine that you are just entering the theater of physical manifestation. You are handed a printed program that portrays the drama of self. Generic man is the star. He plays the part of Stanley Self-Image (or Sara Self-Image, as the case may be.) Read your program and note the acts through which Stanley passes in the drama of life:

## PROGRAM

### DRAMA OF LIFE
*A Play in Three Parts*

Author _____ A. Wonderful Cause
Director _____ Magic Mind
That Great Director of
**WORLD PLAYS, INC.**

### PRESENTING

Those Stars of Stage, Screen and All-A-Vision
*STANLEY AND SARA SELF-IMAGE*

### ACT I
The opening scene depicts a misty land of pristine beauty. Here first cause has brought forth in evolutionary order each of its expressions, culminating in the finest representation of itself, the self-aware beings played by Stanley and Sara. They are free, joyous, perfect representations of life itself.

### ACT II
The second scene opens with Stanley and Sara plodding through a dull daily routine. The laughter is gone from their lips, and their shoulders are stooped from the burdens they bear. Lines of discouragement and worry show on their faces.

231

Their eyelids seem heavy. Can it be that they are drugged? Can it be that they are asleep to their potentialities?

## ACT III

The third scene portrays Stanley and Sara in their mature years, yet they appear youthful and alive. Their faces are wreathed in smiles. The stamp of success is upon their features, their affairs, and the interior harmony of their lives. Their eyes are bright with the vision of all the universe holds for them.

Put yourself in the place of Stanley or Sara in the above program and determine which act you are now playing. If you are bogged down in Act II, if life seems dull and impoverished, then awaken to your potentialities and move on to Act III. The universal drama itself is a success. It is a hit that has never folded. Although some of its actors have lacked skill, the drama is enduring enough to survive and allow each actor to rise to success.

No one can question the bright destiny of the universal drama of life. Looking back along the evolutionary trail, it is evident that every successful experiment in the drama was retained and extended. From the amoeba to man, we witness the successful march of life. Like a stage play, with every rehearsal something of value was added. And it is this value which, elaborated upon, finally culminated in the marvelous body and mind of man.

You are a participant in the greatest of all plays. It is having a long and successful engagement. The longer the run, the more exciting does the play become. Greater diversity and interest are generated as the thought of man, written into the script of experience, is produced upon the stage of life—the physical world.

### Act I—The setting for the play

Read again Act I in the above program. Visualize the

scope of the universal drama as first-cause pushes itself forth into form. Consider how the stage was set for man long before he stepped out upon it. Contingencies and needs were provided for before they arose. All the stage props were readied far in advance. Life began preparing for man's success millions of years ago.

As man awakened to the wisdom of building permanent shelter, timber and stone were there to supply his needs. When the time came that he found it more convenient to stay in one area and grow his food instead of hunting it, man found soil enriched through the eons with humus. When needed for warmth and the working of metals, man discovered the waiting coal. Later he found oil sealed in the bowels of the earth to fulfill his needs for transportation fuel. Through millenniums of time, nuclear energy has been awaiting the conscious call of man. In addition to all this, life has supplied man with the deductive, analytical, inquiring, restless mind that impels him to explore the potentialities awaiting him. Millions, yes billions, of years of preparation have gone into programming your life for success!

## Act II—The side show within life's drama

In Act II of the Drama of Life, the direction of the play is relegated to the individual actor. Universal-cause authors the drama and plans the direction down to the point where man emerges as a self-aware being. Here, the direction that has been universal becomes personalized and individually staged. In the second act, the individual carries on his own sideshow within life's all-encompassing drama. He becomes responsible for staging and interpreting the action. His efforts may be bungling and slow. He may be asleep to his potentialities. But eventually, through trial and error, Stanley (or Sara, as is the case) will come into a realization of the powers inherent in him.

## Act III—Awakening to life's potential

When man realizes that he is not a victim of the drama in which he features but is co-director, he is freed from the dull, uncreative sideshow he carried on within the magnificent drama of life. A new feeling of power and command surges up within him, and he knows he has the skill to fulfill the original script. He throws away the altered and mutilated program he used in the second act and awakens to his role as joint actor-director of his life. This, you can do also! Learn to direct your daily drama by processing your mind with positive ideas and self-conceptions. Assume command as director and rise to the high potentials intended for you from the beginning.

Now, use Mental Data Processing Card No. 22 to bring your individual role into alignment with the universal success program inherent in life:

I now assert my authority as actor-director of the drama of life and claim the success role intended for me. I reject the altered script that has cast me as inadequate and limited. In its place, I fulfill the uniquely perfect and special role life has prepared for me down through the eons.

*Mental Data Processing Card No. 22*

### Portrait of a successful failure

This has been called the age of specialization. There are specialists in all branches of service to mankind— in the medical field, in science, in the arts, and in all walks of life. Specialization enables the individual to demonstrate a mastery in his chosen field that he could not attain if he tried to cover too large an area.

The person who specializes in order to achieve success is one thing, but what of the person who specializes in failure? Frances was such a specialist! It could even be said that she had gained mastery in her field. She was a master at misery and demonstrated great success at it.

She was superbly successful at being unhappy. All of the forces of life seemed to conspire against her. Regardless of what happened to her, whether it was an act of nature or an act of man, she was critical of it. Everything added to her burden of unhappiness. If it rained, she was depressed. If it didn't rain, the dryness gave her cause for complaint. Rain aggravated her rheumatism. Dryness irritated her sinuses. She always seemed to have a problem to fit the occasion.

Frances had achieved as high a measure of success at being unhappy as anyone could. She did so not knowing that one of the simple yet basic laws of mental cybernetics is that *life is always successful*. Hence, *a person succeeds at whatever he attempts, be it success or failure!*

## Mind knows nothing of failure

Mind achieves what it is programmed to express. It knows nothing of failure. It knows only how to obey the commands it receives. History is replete with accounts of those who have achieved a high level of success in some area of life. Familiar to all are the names of men like Carnegie, Rockefeller, Edison, Ford and others who started on the bottom rung and worked their way to the top. Their success is exciting and inspiring, and you can learn much by studying the thought techniques they used. Mind, acting upon the success command given it by such men, obeyed and successfully produced fame for them. But what of the legions of people who are failures? What thought techniques did they use to make their demonstrations? Although less inspiring, you can learn what to avoid by studying the attitudes, the self-appraisals, and feelings that constitute the program which successfully produced the failure they had achieved!

A basic understanding of mental cybernetics is that a universal law outpictures and brings to fruition the subjective programming of mind, be it success-oriented or failure-bound. The dominant nature of man's consciousness becomes a goal toward which he moves. If his dominant tone (or mental program) is one of failure, then the individual moves successfully toward failure!

Dr. Ernest Holmes in *The Science of Mind says,* "It follows that if we believe that it [law] will not work, it really works by appearing to not work. When we believe that it cannot and will not, then, according to the principle, it does not. But when it does not, it still does—only it does according to our belief that it will not." [2]

Life never fails, but the individual may fail in giving right direction to universal mind. This was the reason why Frances had become such a successful failure. She had directed her life unerringly to a state of failure, due to her critical, fault-finding, complaining attitude of mind.

### How to benefit from the affirmative nature of the subconscious

Frequently the individual is not aware of the part he plays in the programming and sustaining of conditions in his life. He mistakenly believes that conditions are of chance creation, not knowing that mind must first be programmed before answers can manifest. Cause and effect, or the program and the performance, are one and the same. Without the program, there can be no performance. Without the cause, there can be no effect, and the effect must reflect the nature of the cause.

In reading of the success of giants in industry, in politics, in science, and in the arts, it is easy enough to grant that study, application, devotion, perseverance, and singleness of vision constitute a program that out-pictures as success. In examining instances of success in your own personal life, it is easy to accept credit for them and the affirmative thinking that produced them. But, when it comes to unfavorable conditions, the individual seems reluctant to accept the possibility that these conditions were on a program he chose. However, if one program can produce success, then it is only reasonable to grant that another program can produce failure.

Yet, both programs are successful, in that the obedient nature of the subconscous mind has acted affirmatively on the data that each program contained.

236

## Specific application of law for success

When failure is demonstrated instead of success, it might appear that the laws of mental cybernetics are not working. But, when they do not, they still do—only they do so according to your belief that they do not. The laws of mind await your use. If you do not use them or if you use them for negative purposes, they appear not to work by producing adverse results.

All of the laws of the universe await conscious use. For instance, the law of electricity existed as fully during the days of Moses as it does today, but before it could produce power or heat, it had to await the development of a scientific awareness capable of channeling it for specific results. In like manner, the law of mind has always existed, but before it can produce specific good, it must await specific use.

Just as man has learned to specialize the laws of nature, so he must learn to specialize the law of mind. For example, man has specialized the law of electricity and uses it now to perform many functions—lighting his home, cooking his food, providing him with power, splitting the atom, etc.

In the field of botany, man has specialized the laws of nature to bring forth new expressions of plant life. Corn, for instance, is the result of specializing the potentialities of maize, and hybrid corn represents further specialization. Most of our vegetables today have been specialized to man's needs through crossfertilization and hybridization. The results have been new and improved strains.

When man turns to the laws of mind and learns to specialize them to his need for self-fulfillment, peace of mind, brotherhood, and understanding, new and improved results will be demonstrated. However, he must consciously and deliberately specify the result he wishes. He must conceive the specific program he wants to manifest, for the law of mind awaits his direction. Until he uses it, it appears not to work.

## Average thoughts produce average results

If you are to program your mind successfully, you

must specialize your life out of the law of averages. The law of averages is simply this: *Average thinking produces average results.* To think along with a group is to experience results belonging to the group thought. To aspire no higher than mass consciousness aspires is to continue to experience what mankind in general experiences. To think along in a confining rut of mediocre ideas is to demonstrate mediocrity.

One of the prime requirements in programming your mind for success is to free your mind from the limiting beliefs of mass thinking. For example, so long as an individual believes he is born to trouble—a deeply subjectified idea in mass mind—he will be heir to trouble. So long as a person feels that the world owes him a living, he will neglect his own power to make a living. So long as an individual believes he cannot rise above his raising, he will be trapped by environment.

You are living in and from an infinite potential. This potential fills the mold of your belief. Your consciousness of success, love, beauty, harmony, right-action, and abundance draws upon this potential power, converting the potential into actual experience. You see in life what you are looking for, and, by your awareness, you provide the size and shape of the belief-container that life must fill for you.

Don't let average thinkers of the world use your mind for average results. Program your mind for the special results that you want to experience!

### Your starting point in success programming

What is the starting point in the programming of mind? It begins in the realization that most of the time you are only aware of your acquired self. At birth, a personality construct begins to unfold according to the mental atmosphere into which you are thrust. Environment, both mental and physical, provides the frame for the self-image of yourself that you begin to paint. The frame determines the size of the picture until the picture—the self-image—bursts the frame by means of self-awakening. Your present self-image, for the most part, is an acquired image. It is the self you acquired through exposure to a

238

certain environment, home life, parents, school experience, peer appraisal, and self-estimate. In all likelihood, your acquired self is something less than the real self deep within you that awaits your discovery. You are asleep to the potentialities of the real self, just as Stanley Self-Image is in Act II of the Drama of Life. Stanley seems drugged or asleep to the potentialities of self-fulfillment.

Remember, it takes an awakening, a realization of your inherent gifts, to become an intelligent co-director in the Drama of Life. This, Stanley does in Act III when he assumes his rightful role as director of his life. Then, he takes command of the stage, no longer willing to accept an inferior role.

Glance back again at the Program for the Drama of Life. Notice the trinitary format of the action, and picture yourself in the role of Stanley or Sara. You are the result of the trinitary action or trinity. You were conceived by first-cause, produced by the creative magic of mind, and now as actor you perform in the spotlight at the center of the stage. You are indispensable to the trinity of author-director-actor shown below:

A. *Wonderful Cause*
    (conceives the drama)＿＿＿＿＿＿AUTHOR
*Magic Mind*
    (produces the drama) ＿＿＿＿＿＿..DIRECTOR
*Stanley* (or Sara, as the case may be)
    (performs the drama) ＿＿＿＿＿＿ACTOR

You are the actor upon the stage of life. This is your role. You cannot assign it to another. No one else can perform it for you. Yet you are also more than the actor, for the directorship of life has been shared with you as Stanley or Sara. You have a part in the further programming, staging, and continued success of the play. In addition to your role as actor and as co-director, you are free to edit the original script of the play of life. How do you do this?

## Reprogramming previous programs

In programming your mind for success, what you have to work with *and all you have to work with* is mind. This mind consists of the dual functions of the conscious and the subconscious—of the volitional and the mechanical—of that which programs and that which is programmed. The subconscious mind is like a computer with unlimited resources of power and intelligence at its disposal. The conscious mind is like the computer programmer whose job it is to choose the data fed into the machine.

Norbert Weiner in *Cybernetics* says, "The ideal computing machine must have all its data inserted at the beginning, and it must be as free as possible from human interference." [3] In comparing the subconscious to a computer, the one element that cannot be met is freedom from human interference. An important difference between a computer and the subconscious mind is this: The computer can be programmed for a single run and then, the data erased. The machine can then be reprogrammed with other data, and other answers will come forth. The subconscious mind, however, receives a continuous stream of data. It is never idle. Data in the subconscious are never completely erased. Therefore, the new programming you do must take place in the midst of previous programs. You can, of course, alter existing programs. And you can begin new programs that supersede old ones.

There is another vital difference between the subconscious and the computer. This concerns the emotional intensity and depth with which a program was originally fed into the subconscious. Some data, with the backing of tradition and religion, are tamped deeply into the subconscious. Hence, feelings of fear, of self-depreciation, of unworthiness and guilt may be deeply entrenched.

## How to program in depth

The mind that is chronically discouraged is programmed for discouragement. The consciousness stamped with a failure pattern is scheduled for failure. The consciousness keypunched with success concepts is programmed for success. However, these programs may not be of equal intensity. Here is another area where the analogy with a computer differs. All data fed into a computer are of equal intensity, but this is not so with the human emotions. A person may generate a feeling of failure that is far stronger than the occasional feeling of success he may muster. Hence, the length of time it takes for success to be demonstrated will depend upon how deep-seated the negative concept of failure is and how long it takes for a new program to alter previous data.

It may logically be said that the more entrenched a self-image is, the more intense must be the data that are to alter it. Surface concepts can be altered more easily than entrenched ones. By the same token, surface images can be induced more quickly. However, they can also be dissipated more easily. To illustrate, a person in the selling field who gets hold of self-help literature on the use of will power may quickly rise to the top. However, he will stay at the top only by means of depth programming as taught by the science of mental cybernetics.

## How to make this and every day successful

Depth programming means every day programming. Programming your mind for success means programming it moment by moment. The reprogramming of your life can appear to be an enormous job unless you handle it a moment at a time. Establish the habit of making each day successful. Program an element of satisfaction, self-fulfillment, creativity, and joy into each day.

It has been said that life by the yard is hard, but by the inch it's a cinch. A person may dream of a successful life but lose sight of the step-by-step experiences that make for success. A successful life is made up of successful days. If you have a predominance of such days, you will have a rich and rewarding life. If your hours are successful, your days will follow suit.

Success is not a magic label you tack onto a completed job; it is an awareness that you experience. For example, let us say that 15 individual things happen to you during a day. If you acted affirmatively toward a majority of these experiences—deriving some measure of value from each one—then the scales for the day are tipped toward success.

However, one event may tend to dominate the day. You may give it greater significance in terms of attention. This is not to say that it may be more valuable; it may have no value at all. But you attend to it more. Let us say that out of the 15 happenings, one was an insult you received from someone. You were hurt and humiliated. If a preponderance of your attention is centered upon this negative experience, it can nullify the other 14 positive events.

Applying this to the weeks, months, and years ahead, if from each day the negative is accentuated, you will have a dismal life. A computer cannot give the data fed into it unequal significance, but you can. By attending to the negative data of the day instead of the positive, you can slant the results produced by the computer of the subconscious. Therefore, you must train yourself to give greatest stress to those things of a positive nature. For to make each separate act a success, is to make the total program a success!

Make this mental cybernetics law a daily rule: *For each pleasant and constructive experience, I shall be grateful. And, from each unpleasant experience, I shall learn—and for that learning I shall be grateful.*

## Summary points in programming your success

*First:* Duplicate paths of thought will lead to duplicated experiences. Corrective programming, then, demands that you depart from the path that the mind normally takes. For instance, if there is a situation in your life that you want to change, it will not be changed by thinking about it in the way you always have. Vernon Howard says in *Psycho-Pictography that* "A problem existing on the level of conditioned thinking cannot be solved by conditioned thinking." [4] To program your mind for success, use data—ideas, plans, attitudes, feelings, visions, and aspirations—that lead you beyond the accustomed view of life to a fresh perspective.

*Second:* Mind power, as it flows through you, is impersonal and undifferentiated. It is pure energy, ready to fill any container or flow through any channel provided. The energy of life does not care what form it takes or how generous or meager the proportions may be. Therefore, the creative energy of the subconscious can be utilized for any specific good toward which you desire to direct it. As water flows in a stream which it carves for itself, so will the energy of life flow in the channel you carve by your own thought. It is your thought that gives direction to the magic of mind.

*Third:* Don't listen to those who are always in the midst of a depression—whatever their particular depression may be. This is not to say that you are to be callous toward those who are in economic straits or toward those who are mentally and physically depressed, but be mindful of the truth that *what gets your mind gets you.* As pointed out before, man should not be so much concerned with getting people out of poverty as he is with getting poverty out of people.

*Fourth:* Become aware that you are a thinking being, with the freedom to change the tenor of your thoughts. To the degree that you change, your experience will change. Become aware that you are master of your thoughts. As you can think only one thought at a time, you can control this one thought. Hence, at this moment, you are in control. You are master of your thoughts. Nothing outside of you has the power to control your mind other than whatever power you permit another person, thing, or condition to exert. Remember, your mind cannot be idle. It is operating constantly. Either you are thinking or someone else is thinking for you. Don't relinquish your right to freedom of thought. In this freedom lies a new life. Take command of this freedom by using your mind creatively and constructively yourself!

*Fifth:* Use Mental Data Processing Card No. 23 to program your life for success.

> Today (and in the days ahead) I specialize the law of mind to my needs by giving it thoughtful direction. I find it easy to control my thoughts, for I handle them one-by-one. I practice depth programming by making each moment a success and letting the days follow suit.

*Mental Data Processing Card No. 23*

# CHAPTER SUMMARY OF POINTS TO PONDER

1. The success stamp of creative mind is imprinted in the heart of everything that lives. Success is a universal fact that can become, and should become, individual experience. You live and move and have your being in a creative intelligence that is ever striving to live more abundantly by means of you.

2. Life loves to express, to flourish, to multiply, to create, to prosper, and to succeed. Hence, life loves a prosperous person. The desire of life for fuller expression is basic to the nature of first-cause. Your desire for success is not individual, but individualized. Life demands success of you!

3. Poverty is a negation of life—whether it exists as poverty of understanding, as nonproductivity, as lack of friends, or as restricted income. Poverty is a negative program that puts the power of the subconscious to work on false data.

4. Life is a success drama that has endured through the ages. It will not end in failure at your door if you align your personal play with the universal drama. To do so, you must give up any inferior side show roles that cast you as a failure.

5. Failure is not real or natural to you. It is not written into the original script by first-cause. Failure is due simply to lack of insight and skill in grasping your starring role in the universal drama.

6. To rise to stardom in the Drama of Life:

   (a) Accept your role as co-author of your personalized play of life and rewrite the script wherever it is unsatisfactory. To do this, use the mental cybernetics techniques described in this book for reprogramming your mind for success.

   (b) Realize that you direct your play through the ideas you think moment by moment through the day. Plan to make each day's performance a success and the weeks and years will, of necessity, be successful.

(c) Understand that the action of the drama (life's experiences) must conform to your self-image. Stanley Self-Image must portray the characterization he has formed of himself. You, too, will experience action that conforms to your mental conception of yourself. Conceive a new self-image, and you will find yourself performing it on the Stage of Life!

# List of References

CHAPTER 1

[1] Hudson, Thomas J., *The Evolution of the Soul*. Chicago: A. C. McClurg & Co., 1904, p. 4.
[2] *The New Chain Reference Bible, King James Version*, Frank C. Thompson, editor. Mt. Morris: Chain-Reference Publishing Co., 1934, Matthew 25:29.
[3] Dunbar, Flanders, *Mind and Body: Psychosomatic Medicine*. New York: Random House, 1955, p. 34.
[4] James, William, *The Principles of Psychology*. Vol. 1 and 2. New York: Dover Publications, Inc., 1950, p. 121.

CHAPTER 2

[1] Emerson, Ralph Waldo, *Emerson's Essays*. Mount Vernon: The Peter Pauper Press, p. 28.
[2] *Ibid.*, p. 7.
[3] *Bible, op. cit.*, Jeremiah 23:36.
[4] *Ibid.*, Proverbs 4:23.

CHAPTER 3

[1] Fitzgerald, Edward, *Rubaiyat of Omar Khayyam*. Philadelphia: David McKay Co., 1942, p. 99.

CHAPTER 4

[1] Emerson, *op. cit.*
[2] *Ibid.*
[3] *Ibid.*
[4] *Bible, op. cit.*, Matthew 7:26.

⁵ Crabbe, George, *The New Dictionary or Thoughts,* Jonathan Edwards and C. N. Catrevas, editors. New York: Standard Book Co., 1954, p. 240.
⁶ Shakespeare, William.

CHAPTER 5

¹ Emerson, *op. cit.,* p. 101.
² Hoyle, Fred, *The Nature of the Universe.* New York: Harper and Row, 1950, p. 122.
³ James, *op. cit.,* p. 450.
⁴ *Webster's Collegiate Dictionary,* Fifth Edition. Springfield: C. & C. Merriam Co., Publishers, 1940, p. 71.

CHAPTER 6

¹ Monteith, A. C. (an official of Westinghouse Corporation), *Quote, The Weekly Digest.*
² *Webster, op. cit.,* p. 497.
³ James, *op. cit.,* p. 402.

CHAPTER 7

¹ *Webster, op. cit.,* p. 503.
² *Ibid.,* p. 312.
³ Hill, Napoleon, *Think and Grow Rich.* New York: Hawthorne Books, Inc., 1966.
⁴ Rittenhouse, Jessie B., "My Wage," from *Door of Dreams.* Boston: Houghton Mifflin Company.
⁵ Hubbard, Elbert, *Quote, The Weekly Digest.*
⁶ *Bible, op. cit.,* II Chronicles 1:10–11.
⁷ *Webster, op. cit.,* p. 257.
⁸ James, *op. cit.*
⁹ *Ibid.*

CHAPTER 8

¹ *Holy Bible, Revised Standard Version.* New York: Thomas Nelson & Sons, 1952, Romans 7:15.
² Fisher, James T. and Lowell S. Hawley, *A Few Buttons Missing: The Casebook of a Psychiatrist.* New York: Medical Publications Limited, 1952, p. 195.
³ *Webster, op. cit.,* p. 205.
⁴ Emerson, *op. cit.,* p. 74.
⁵ Emerson, *The New Dictionary of Thoughts, op. cit.,* p. 644.
⁶ Snider, Arthur J., *The Denver Post.* Denver, Colorado.

CHAPTER 9

[1] *Bible, op. cit.,* Psalms 18:26.
[2] *Ibid.,* Luke 15:20.
[3] *Webster, op. cit.,* p. 52.
[4] Alcott, A. B., *The New Dictionary of Thoughts, op. cit.,* p. 646.
[5] *Webster, op. cit.,* p. 1208.
[6] *Bible, op. cit.,* Ecclesiastes 3:1.
[7] *Ibid.,* Proverbs 27:18.
[8] *Webster, op. cit.,* p. 192.
[9] *Ibid.,* p. 342.

CHAPTER 10

[1] Emerson, *op. cit.*
[2] Schwartz, David. J., *The Magic of Psychic Power.* West Nyack: Parker Publishing Co., Inc., 1965, p. 216.
[3] Hutchnecker, Arnold, *The Will to Live.* New York: Prentice-Hall, Inc., 1966, p. 129.
[4] Haddock, Frank Channing, *The Power of Will.* Tarrytown: The Book of Destiny, 1961., p. 71.
[5] James, *op. cit.*
[6] Englebardt, Stanley, *Computers.* New York: Pyramid Publications, Inc, 1962, p. 140.
[7] Wilson, Margery, *Kinetic Psycho-Dynamics.* Englewood Cliffs: Prentice-Hall, Inc., 1963, p. 84.
[8] Haddock, *op. cit.,* p. 113.

CHAPTER 11

[1] *Bible, Revised Standard Version,* Isaiah 38:16.
[2] Wheeler, Elmer, *How to Sell Yourself to Others.* New York: Prentice-Hall, Inc., 1947, p. 99.
[3] Rhine, Joseph Banks, *New World of the Mind,* New York: William Sloane Associates, 1953.
[4] Street, J. C., *Hidden Ways Across the Threshold.* London: William Rider & Son, Ltd., 1887, p. 137.
[5] Bible, Genesis 13:14–17.

CHAPTER 12

[1] Englebardt, *op. cit.,* p. 8.
[2] Holmes, Ernest, *The Science of Mind.* New York: Dodd, Mead and Company, 1958, p. 52.
[3] Wiener, Norbert, *Cybernetics: Or Control and Communication in the Animal and the Machine.* Cambridge: The M. I. T. Press, 1961, p. 118.
[4] Howard, Vernon, *Psycho-Pictography.* West Nyack: Parker Publishing Company, 1965, p. 35.

248

# INDEX

250

251

254